OTHER TITLES IN THE GREENHAVEN PRESS LITERARY COMPANION SERIES:

AMERICAN AUTHORS

Maya Angelou
Stephen Crane
Emily Dickinson
William Faulkner
F. Scott Fitzgerald
Robert Frost
Nathaniel Hawthorne
Ernest Hemingway
Herman Melville
Arthur Miller
Flannery O'Connor
Eugene O'Neill
Edgar Allan Poe
John Steinbeck
Mark Twain
Walt Whitman
Thornton Wilder

AMERICAN LITERATURE

The Adventures of
  Huckleberry Finn
The Adventures of Tom
  Sawyer
Black Boy
The Call of the Wild
The Catcher in the Rye
The Crucible
Death of a Salesman
Fahrenheit 451
A Farewell to Arms
The Glass Menagerie
The Grapes of Wrath
The Great Gatsby
Heart of Darkness
My Antonia
Of Mice and Men
The Old Man and the Sea
The Pearl
One Flew Over the Cuckoo's
  Nest
Our Town
The Pearl
A Raisin in the Sun
The Scarlet Letter
A Separate Peace
To Kill a Mockingbird

THE GREENHAVEN PRESS
Literary Companion
TO AMERICAN LITERATURE

READINGS ON

THE RED PONY

Clarice Swisher, *Book Editor*

David L. Bender, *Publisher*
Bruno Leone, *Executive Editor*
Bonnie Szumski, *Series Editor*

Greenhaven Press, Inc., San Diego, CA

Every effort has been made to trace the owners of copyrighted material. The articles in this volume may have been edited for content, length, and/or reading level. The titles have been changed to enhance the editorial purpose. Those interested in locating the original source will find the complete citation on the first page of each article.

Library of Congress Cataloging-in-Publication Data

Readings on The red pony / Clarice Swisher, book editor.
    p.   cm. — (The Greenhaven Press literary
companion to American literature)
    Includes bibliographical references and index.
    ISBN 0-7377-0192-7 (pbk. : alk. paper) —
ISBN 0-7377-0193-5 (lib. bdg. : alk. paper)
    1. Steinbeck, John, 1902–1968. Red pony. 2. Boys in
literature. I. Swisher, Clarice, 1933–   II. Series.

PS3537.T3234 R437   2001
813'.52—dc21   00-037667

Cover photo: Archive Photos

Copyright © 2001 by Greenhaven Press, Inc.
PO Box 289009
San Diego, CA 92198-9009
Printed in the U.S.A.

> "The Red Pony *was written a long time ago, when there was desolation in my family. The first death had occurred. And the family, which every child believes to be immortal, was shattered. . . . The first tortured question 'why?' and then acceptance and then the child becomes anew.* The Red Pony *was an attempt, an experiment if you wish, to set down this loss and acceptance and growth."*
>
> —*John Steinbeck*

CONTENTS

Foreword   9

Introduction   11

John Steinbeck: A Biography   12

Characters and Plot   28

Chapter 1: Major Themes in *The Red Pony*

1. The Importance of the Salinas Valley Setting
by Freeman Champney   35
Knowledge of the Salinas Valley is necessary to understand
Steinbeck's works. Steinbeck depicts in intimate detail the
valley's lush beauty and its harsh rocky mountains in
addition to discussing the area's business and industry.

2. Charles Darwin and Steinbeck's Ideal Hero
by Brian E. Railsback   39
From a biological point of view, John Steinbeck and
Charles Darwin agree on the traits that set people apart
from other creatures and make them most human. In *The
Red Pony* Billy Buck comes close to evolving into the ideal
hero.

3. Group Theory in "The Leader of the People"
by Richard Astro   46
Steinbeck and his friend, marine biologist Edward F.
Ricketts, studied the way humans and animals act in
groups. Though human groups are like animal groups in
some ways, humans can be distinguished by their spirit
and their ability to derive meaning.

4. The Theme of Life and Death
by Arnold L. Goldsmith   51
The four stories in *The Red Pony* cover two years in the life
of Jody Tiflin, during which he matures when forced to
accept the realities of death.

5. The Ambiguous Role of Nature *by Richard E. Hart*   57
Steinbeck presents a complex view of humans in relation to
nature. At times he portrays humans as cogs in an

indifferent nature; at others he portrays humans asserting their free will against nature's forces. Both views are illustrated in *The Red Pony.*

Chapter 2: Characters in *The Red Pony*

1. The Education of a Young Boy *by Peter Lisca*   63
Jody learns about the nature of death—violent, calm, and life-giving—in the first three stories. In the fourth he learns the value of history from his grandfather's stories of the past.

2. Jody's Initiation into Adulthood
by F.W. Watt   69
The events of *The Red Pony* revolve around Jody's initiation into adulthood.

3. The Role of Billy Buck *by Robert M. Benton*   73
Jody learns about life from his natural surroundings and from nature's events of birth and death. Most directly, however, he learns from Billy Buck, a man who represents the union of man with nature.

Chapter 3: *The Red Pony:* Narrative Structure and Style

1. Narrative Technique in *The Red Pony*
by Howard Levant   79
Steinbeck tells the stories from Jody's point of view, and Jody's own storytelling reveals his growing awareness of important life lessons—that humans are imperfect and that tragedy and death are inevitable parts of life.

2. Structural Patterns Unify *The Red Pony*
by John H. Timmerman   90
Though each story in *The Red Pony* tells a separate episode in Jody's life, the book is unified by Jody's ongoing rebellion against his father, recurring tensions and dreams, and continued maturation.

3. Steinbeck's Mature Style in *The Red Pony*
by Harry Thornton Moore   104
Though the stories in *The Red Pony* were written early in Steinbeck's career, they manifest a mature style, particularly in his depiction of ranch life in the Salinas Valley and his creation of characters.

4. A New Style in *The Red Pony* *by Randolph Bartlett* 108
With the 1937 edition of *The Red Pony*, Steinbeck writes in a new refined style suitable for the subtle themes in the Jody stories. His style has force and conveys close familiarity with the setting, a young boy, and animals.

5. Steinbeck Praised as a Short-Story Writer
by Jay Parini   110

The Red Pony was first published with only three stories. In 1938 Steinbeck added "The Leader of the People" and published the four-story version in the collection, *The Long Valley*. Though this collection received glowing reviews and made the best-seller list, Steinbeck was more interested in his novels than his short stories.

Chapter 4: *The Red Pony* on Film

1. *The Red Pony* Adapted for Film
by Joseph R. Millichap   114

The film version of *The Red Pony* uses material primarily from two of the stories. Much simpler and less realistic than the written version, the film is less effective in recounting Jody's maturation process.

2. *The Red Pony* as Story Cycle and Film
by Warren French   126

John Steinbeck wrote the script for the film *The Red Pony*, an unusual practice for the author of a book. His film script, focusing on "The Gift" and using only parts of two other stories, is a simpler sequence with a revised happy ending suitable for a preadolescent audience.

Chronology   141

For Further Research   146

Index   148

FOREWORD

The story's bare facts are simple: The captain, an old and scarred seafarer, walks with a peg leg made of whale ivory. He relentlessly drives his crew to hunt the world's oceans for the great white whale that crippled him. After a long search, the ship encounters the whale and a fierce battle ensues. Finally the captain drives his harpoon into the whale, but the harpoon line catches the captain about the neck and drags him to his death.

A simple story, a straightforward plot—yet, since the 1851 publication of Herman Melville's *Moby-Dick*, readers and critics have found many meanings in the struggle between Captain Ahab and the whale. To some, the novel is a cautionary tale that depicts how Ahab's obsession with revenge leads to his insanity and death. Others believe that the whale represents the unknowable secrets of the universe and that Ahab is a tragic hero who dares to challenge fate by attempting to discover this knowledge. Perhaps Melville intended Ahab as a criticism of Americans' tendency to become involved in well-intentioned but irrational causes. Or did Melville model Ahab after himself, letting his fictional character express his anger at what he perceived as a cruel and distant god?

Although literary critics disagree over the meaning of *Moby-Dick*, readers do not need to choose one particular interpretation in order to gain an understanding of Melville's novel. Instead, by examining various analyses, they can gain numerous insights into the issues that lie under the surface of the basic plot. Studying the writings of literary critics can also aid readers in making their own assessments of *Moby-Dick* and other literary works and in developing analytical thinking skills.

The Greenhaven Literary Companion Series was created with these goals in mind. Designed for young adults, this unique anthology series provides an engaging and comprehensive introduction to literary analysis and criticism. The essays included in the Literary Companion Series are chosen for their accessibility to a young adult audience and are expertly edited in consideration of both the reading and comprehension levels of this audience. In addition, each essay is introduced by a concise summation that presents the contributing writer's main themes and insights. Every anthology in the Literary Companion Series contains a varied selection of critical essays that cover a wide time span and express diverse views. Wherever possible, primary sources are represented through excerpts from authors' notebooks, letters, and journals and through contemporary criticism.

Each title in the Literary Companion Series pays careful consideration to the historical context of the particular author or literary work. In-depth biographies and detailed chronologies reveal important aspects of authors' lives and emphasize the historical events and social milieu that influenced their writings. To facilitate further research, every anthology includes primary and secondary source bibliographies of articles and/or books selected for their suitability for young adults. These engaging features make the Greenhaven Literary Companion series ideal for introducing students to literary analysis in the classroom or as a library resource for young adults researching the world's great authors and literature.

Exceptional in its focus on young adults, the Greenhaven Literary Companion Series strives to present literary criticism in a compelling and accessible format. Every title in the series is intended to spark readers' interest in leading American and world authors, to help them broaden their understanding of literature, and to encourage them to formulate their own analyses of the literary works that they read. It is the editors' hope that young adult readers will find these anthologies to be true companions in their study of literature.

Introduction

John Steinbeck's *The Red Pony,* a collection of four stories about a young boy named Jody, is a wonderful introduction for young readers to the study of serious literature. The loosely connected episodes tell a simple, engaging story with many literary devices apparent enough for the novice to see, such as unity of setting, recurring events, symbols, and imagery. The collected stories raise relevant questions about life and death and justice that are bound to trigger discussion among young readers.

The Red Pony is also an adult book. At first glance, the simplicity disguises Steinbeck's carefully crafted style and structure: he depicts both characters and setting in minimalist strokes and evokes universal and philosophical issues, such as the reality of life's cycles and the mysterious connections unifying humans, animals, and nature, that are embedded within the simple story. Under close observation, these elements challenge the mature reader. For the reader of any sophistication, *The Red Pony* is a good read, filled with suspense and powerful emotion.

When the first three stories were published in 1937, critics recognized a new style in Steinbeck's writing. "The Leader of the People" appeared as part of *The Red Pony* for the first time in 1938 when it was included in a collection of stories called *The Long Valley,* which made the best-seller list and received glowing reviews. In 1945 the four stories appeared in an illustrated publication. The film version, for which Steinbeck wrote the script, is based primarily on "The Gift" and one other story; for the expected preadolescent audience, he created a new happy ending. This profound story of a boy's confrontations with the realities of life continues to fascinate young and old readers alike.

JOHN STEINBECK: A BIOGRAPHY

Like Jody in *The Red Pony*, "Steinbeck had places of his own, places tucked in among the wooded, brushy banks of nearby drainage ditches, places where he could sit and dream and watch the movements of the birds and small animals," reports Jackson J. Benson in *The True Adventures of John Steinbeck, Writer.* Steinbeck grew up in the small town of Salinas, California, the surrounding valley, and the nearby Pacific coastal towns of Monterey and Pacific Grove, the settings of many of his best works. In looking back, Steinbeck said about the Salinas Valley, "I can remember my childhood names for grasses and secret flowers. I remember where a toad may live and what time the birds awaken in the summer—and what trees and seasons smelled like." From his early years, he had a connection with nature.

John Ernst Steinbeck was born on February 27, 1902, in Salinas, the third child of John Ernst Sr. and Olivia Hamilton Steinbeck. John had two sisters, Esther, born in 1892, and Elizabeth (Beth), born in 1894. John Sr., a gentle, shy, remote man of German descent, ran a flour-milling business until it failed in 1910; after a period of disappointment and despondency, he became the treasurer of Monterey County, a respected and financially secure post. The Steinbecks lived in a large Victorian house on Central Avenue and took an active part in community and cultural life. Steinbeck's mother, called Olive, grew up on the Hamilton ranch sixty miles south of Salinas and lived there while she received an education qualifying her to teach elementary school. In *John Steinbeck: A Biography*, Jay Parini describes how the ranch influenced Steinbeck:

> Steinbeck spent a lot of time there as a child, often following in his grandfather's large bootstops as he went about his daily chores; it was on the Hamilton ranch that he learned so many of the practical things that stuck with him throughout his life. The routine of farm work—and the ethos of practicality that inevitably goes with it—hung brilliantly in his imagination

and became an essential part of his way of being. . . . [Moreover] the Hamilton ranch became a vital part of his personal story about himself, and it would reappear many times in his fiction, as in the Tiflin ranch in *The Red Pony.*

Besides the Hamilton ranch, the small cottage Steinbeck's father bought on Eleventh Street in Pacific Grove near Monterey became for Steinbeck a special retreat during weekends and summer holidays. The family packed into the horse-drawn surrey for the rough trip to the coast, stopping always for roadside picnics and play for the children. Steinbeck's sister Beth recalls, "The place was always a lucky place for us. . . . John and I often talked about those rides." Like the Hamilton ranch, these coastal spots appear in Steinbeck's books. Parini explains:

> The bouldery and brilliant shoreline along the Monterey coast became a favorite haunt of young Steinbeck, who in *Travels with Charley*, his last major book, recalled that he "grew up on its shore, collected marine animals along the coast." In *Tortilla Flat* he offers a vivid sketch of the town and its setting: "Monterey sits on the slope of a hill, with a blue bay below it and with a forest of tall dark pine trees at its back." Famous in Steinbeck's day for sardine canneries, which crowded along the shore, Monterey became a setting for several of Steinbeck's best-known novels and stories, and it became for him a sacred place that he returned to in difficult periods throughout his life.

> Not half a mile from the town, the coastline becomes one of the most spectacular in California, with its steep cliffs and rocky shingle. Kelp and bladder wrack swirl in brilliant colors in rock pools. Priestly gulls hang in the wind over brilliant stretches of blue-green water, and there are long strands of bone-white beach. Steinbeck fell in love with the smell of the sea, the wet rocks and kelp, the sharpness of iodine and the odor of the washed, crumbling calcareous shells.

Both the ranch and the seaside setting instilled in Steinbeck an important element in his education—a familiarity with and love of nature.

EARLY CULTURAL AND INTELLECTUAL TRAINING

Before he entered school, Steinbeck had become a confident reader, but he had also become timid and shy. The failure of his father's business and his resulting depression and withdrawal had a profound effect on the young boy. Moreover, he was self-conscious about his looks; Parini describes Steinbeck, even as a boy, with "bulbous nose and heavy brow, the long (and later craggy) face and massive ears that folded out like flaps, the swollen chest and long, spindly legs." When children teased him about his physical features and his behavior, he withdrew into books and daydreams. His mother, who responded by coddling him, undermined his confidence. To counter Olive's effect, his father spent time with his son every day on the farm doing chores. He bought John a pony named Jill and expected his son to care for it.

Steinbeck did well in elementary school. For a time each summer, he was sent to visit Aunt Molly, Olive's sister, for further exposure to literature and music, but as he grew older, Steinbeck wanted to roam the hills and fields and felt confined by the lessons. Aunt Molly influenced him in another way, when she gave him a book. Years after, he wrote about the gift:

> One day, an aunt gave me a book and fatuously ignored my resentment. I stared at the black print with hatred, and then gradually the pages opened and let me in. The magic happened. The Bible and Shakespeare and *Pilgrim's Progress* belonged to everyone. But this was mine—secretly mine. It was a cut version of the Caxton "Morte d'Arthur" of Thomas Malory. I loved the old spelling of the words—and the words no longer used. Perhaps a passionate love for the English language opened to me from this one book. I was delighted to find out paradoxes—that "cleave" means both to stick together and to cut apart. . . . For a long time, I had a secret language.

With his younger sister, Mary, born in 1909, John read the Arthurian tales, acted them out, and searched for the Grail with the pony Jill.

SHYNESS AND REBELLION

During his West End Grammar School years from fourth through eighth grades, John explored and made friends. As a fourth grader he was known to disrupt the class, but by fifth grade, though he was still shy and often a loner, he demonstrated the proper behavior expected of him. He made two good friends, Glenn Graves and Max Wagner, and found he could gain their admiration by telling stories. He had a paper route and went exploring alone on his bicycle to the local Chinatown, the Mexican neighborhoods, and the outlying ranches and pastures. On these trips he gathered in sights and sounds used in his stories.

In 1915, Steinbeck began ninth grade in Salinas High School, where he followed a regular college-preparatory program of English, mathematics, science, history, and foreign languages. He was neither popular with other students nor a remarkable student. Classmates found his personality erratic, either very friendly or hostile, and teachers, who thought his features gave him a stupid look, made fun of him in front of their classes. Steinbeck reacted with silent, burning shame. During his junior year, he secretly began writing stories and sending them anonymously to magazines; near the end of his junior year, however, he contracted pneumonia and pleurisy which interrupted his school and his writing. Antibiotics had yet to be discovered, so the illness was serious, requiring surgery to remove a rib and infected tissue. The illness helped him mature and take seriously his senior year during which he studied, became president of the student body, joined the science and drama clubs, and edited the yearbook, activities that helped him feel less shy. He graduated in a class of twenty-four students.

Steinbeck entered Stanford University in 1919, registered as a liberal arts student. With new surroundings and in competition with Stanford students, John's feelings of ineptness and timidity arose again; he coped by withdrawing instead of trying, by acting disruptive, and by taking on eccentric roles. His roommate and good friend, George Mors, a self-directed engineering student, tried to persuade Steinbeck to attend to his studies. When Steinbeck left Stanford with an illness before the spring term of his first year ended, he had earned three credits for the year. He attended Stanford on and off for six years between 1919 and 1925, with fruitful terms in 1923 and 1924 when he took his classes seriously, studied, and earned good grades.

During summers and periods away from Stanford, Steinbeck spent time as a laborer. He worked for a sugar-beet company, Spreckels Sugar, harvesting beets in the fields with migrants and living with them in the bunkhouse. Other times he worked for just over thirty-two cents an hour as a bench chemist, where he ran routine tests on the sugar harvest. In the summer of 1923 he and his sister Mary took a course from C.V. Taylor at the Hopkins Marine Station in Pacific Grove, Stanford's laboratory for the study of marine life. The class observed marine creatures in their natural habitat of Monterey Bay, already familiar to Steinbeck. Parini says, "This period at the marine station laid the basis for his lifelong interest in marine biology and prepared the way for his later friendship with Edward Ricketts." Though Steinbeck appeared aimless during these years, he was absorbing impressions of people and places, filing away details, and trying to work out a style of expression for the stories he wanted to write. He wanted a method to express the unique qualities of people he met on the streets and people from his past.

SEARCHING FOR A VOICE AND A STYLE

Though his years at Stanford never gained him a degree, the time there had several favorable outcomes for Steinbeck. During his sophomore year, he wrote five or six stories about college life, two of which appeared in the *Spectator,* the college literary magazine. When he enrolled in 1924, he was older than his classmates, more confident, and took on the image of diligent scholar with pipe and cloth bookbag. He met several people who became influential in his life. Duke Sheffield was a fellow writer and the two offered each other critical and personal support. Teacher Edith Mirrielees, an "odd, prissy, little old-fashioned" woman whom Steinbeck admired because she "knew what she was talking about," taught a short-story class Steinbeck attended. Though Steinbeck was her star pupil, "he never got more than a B from her," according to Benson. At the English Club, an organization for literature students, Steinbeck met Elizabeth Smith, a middle-aged eccentric member who published stories. She liked Steinbeck's writing, encouraged him to expand his story "A Lady in Infra-Red" into a novel, and let him work in the writing studio built behind her house. Both Mirrielees and Smith urged Steinbeck to stay in school.

After dropping out in 1926, Steinbeck lived in the family cottage in Pacific Grove and tried to make progress on a novel called *A Pot of Gold.* Failing to write anything to his satisfaction, he took a job on a freighter and went, via the Panama Canal, to New York, where his sister Elizabeth lived with her husband. In New York City, he worked first as a construction worker and later as a reporter for a Hearst newspaper for twenty-five dollars a week. A former Stanford friend, Ted Miller, offered to show Steinbeck's stories to publishers, and when one expressed interest, Steinbeck produced nine new stories; however, by the time he had them ready, no publisher would look at them.

Steinbeck returned to California by freighter and found a job as caretaker on the estate of Mrs. Alice Brigham in the Sierra Mountains near Lake Tahoe. This resort area swarmed with vacationers in the summer, but it was deserted in winter, giving Steinbeck solitude and time for reflection. Parini describes the effect:

> The physical isolation of Tahoe provided just the atmosphere
> he needed. He had tried the opposite tack the year before, in
> Manhattan, where the mass of humanity offered a gigantic
> distraction, and a million voices challenged his own. Now, by
> the shores of Tahoe, he had only the wind in the high fir trees
> to compete with the sound of his inner voice, and he had all
> the time in the world to discover his inner voice. . . . Steinbeck
> discovered during this period of isolation in the Tahoe region
> that his artistic nature was such that he could create only in
> solitude; indeed, whenever he listened too much to the voices
> that crowded around him, he became distracted, depressed,
> uncomfortable, barren.

He struggled with large philosophical questions and their
implications for his work. Should he try to write stories with
grand action and bigger-than-life characters, on the order of
the Arthurian stories he had loved in his youth? He ques-
tioned the place of humans as individuals and how they were
forced to comply with a powerful social order. He wondered
if humans were trapped between their animal impulses and
the rules imposed on them by their minds. And he was both-
ered by the poor and hungry people he had seen in the land
of American plenty. These issues would become the founda-
tion on which he would write stories.

Living alone in the caretaker's cottage, he also wrote short
stories, and in 1927 *Smoker's Companion* published one,
"The Gifts of Ivan," under the pseudonym John Stein. By February 1928, though Steinbeck had finished *A Pot of Gold*, he
felt at twenty-six like a failure for having accomplished nothing in his life. In April, he bought an old car for forty dollars
and brought his manuscript of *A Pot of Gold* to Elizabeth
Smith and Edith Mirrielees at Stanford, who encouraged him
to send it to publishers. He changed the title to *A Cup of Gold*,
as Smith suggested, and sent the handwritten manuscript to
Ted Miller in New York, but publishers refused to read a
manuscript that was not typed. By this time Steinbeck was
back at Lake Tahoe, where he had met a vacationing secretary named Carol Henning, who offered to type for him. *A
Cup of Gold* was accepted in January 1929 and brought
Steinbeck four hundred dollars.

FRIENDS AND A WIFE

Steinbeck left Lake Tahoe late in 1929 to visit Carol Henning
in San Francisco, where she had returned after her vacation.
A former Stanford writing friend, Carl Wilhelmson, had a
small apartment there and let Steinbeck stay with him. At the

time Steinbeck was having trouble with a book called *To an Unknown God* and was also working on a book about poor farmers. To help him survive, his parents provided him an income of twenty-five dollars a month so that he could devote his energy to writing.

In San Francisco, he and Carol fell in love; they married in Glendale, near Los Angeles, on January 14, 1930, bought a Belgian shepherd puppy, and soon settled in Pacific Grove, where Carol took a job with the Chamber of Commerce. Because Steinbeck was still getting nothing but rejection slips from publishers, they needed her income and the monthly gift from the Steinbecks. Books sales of all kinds had slumped when the depression hit New York publishing circles.

Just when Steinbeck needed inspiration, he met Edward F. Ricketts, a marine biologist who operated a laboratory and biological-supply company in Monterey near the docks. In *John Steinbeck and Edward Ricketts: The Shaping of a Novelist*, Richard Astro describes their friendship:

> According to Steinbeck, he and Ricketts met in a dentist's waiting room in 1930. Supposedly each had heard of the other, and they struck up an immediate friendship. According to virtually everyone who knew Steinbeck and Ricketts and is willing to talk about the friendship, theirs was a very unique relationship. Steinbeck felt extremely close to Ricketts and needed and desired his companionship, and Ricketts poured out to Steinbeck what, for lack of a better term, must be called love.

Both Steinbeck and Ricketts were witty, cynical risk takers. Ricketts was a confident, intelligent man who could bring order to a confusion of ideas, a skill Steinbeck did not have. The two men frequented the saloons along the docks in a section of Monterey called Cannery Row, spending long hours discussing philosophical and literary ideas and observing the dockworkers. Ricketts advocated a scientific approach to writing; a writer, he told Steinbeck, must be "a scientist of the imagination." Besides their socializing, both men worked hard. With struggle, Steinbeck finished *To an Unknown God* and *Pastures of Heaven,* but he was still unsuccessful in selling either book or any of his stories.

By 1932, Steinbeck's financial situation had worsened. Carol had tried two business ventures that failed and needed emotional support, and Steinbeck was feeling guilty about his failure as a provider. His friend Carl Wilhelmson suggested that Steinbeck hire a New York agent to sell his manuscripts and recommended Mavis McIntosh and Elizabeth Otis, who agreed to take him on as a client. Soon they sold *Pastures of Heaven,* a novel about a family living under a curse, to an American subsidiary of a prestigious British firm; with the sale came a contract for two more novels. Steinbeck set to work to rewrite *To an Unknown God* and changed the title to *To a God Unknown* at Ricketts's suggestion. Reviews of *Pastures of Heaven* were negative and sales limited, a disappointment that meant Steinbeck would receive no further royalties. Concurrently, the British publisher withdrew his contract for two novels because the company was in financial trouble.

CHANGES IN STEINBECK'S FORTUNE

In May 1932, Steinbeck's mother had a stroke and had to be hospitalized. While caring for his ailing parents, Steinbeck began work on two new titles. Stories his father told him gave him the idea for *The Red Pony.* Stories from Susan Gregory, a Monterey high school teacher interested in poor Mexicans called *paisanos,* gave him the idea for *Tortilla Flat.* By 1933 the publishing company had recovered enough financial stability to publish *To a God Unknown,* and in the same year the *North American Review,* a respected literary magazine, published two of the pony stories. In 1934, the *North American Review* published "The Murder," for which Steinbeck won the O. Henry Award for the best story of the year. He was happy that his writing career seemed to be improving, but saddened by his mother's death on February 19, 1934.

Steinbeck's writing style changed as he incorporated Ricketts's suggestions and as he became interested in the theme of social protest. He based *Tortilla Flat* on the Arthur legends, but at the same time took an approach closer to naturalism; that is, he treated his subject more as a scientist treats his evidence, the approach suggested by Ricketts. He sent the manuscript to McIntosh and Otis. Wasting no time, Steinbeck wrote "The Raid," about labor organizers, and a longer work on the same subject, *In Dubious Battle.* A surprise letter came to Steinbeck from a man named Ben Abramson, a bookseller in Chicago, who liked the red pony stories and had been recommending *To a God Unknown* and *Pastures from Heaven* to his customers.

Steinbeck's best news came from Pascal Covici, a New York publisher, in January 1935. Covici offered to publish *Tortilla Flat,* asked to be Steinbeck's exclusive publisher, and wanted to reissue Steinbeck's previous books. Covici published *Tortilla Flat,* which came out in May 1935, a few days after the death of Steinbeck's father; its fine line drawings and effective advance publicity gained the attention of American readers who liked the colorful story and identified with its underdog characters. Soon it was on the best-seller list, making Steinbeck famous, and was nominated for the California Commonwealth Club's gold medal for the best book about California. At first the Monterey Chamber of Commerce expressed disapproval of the book as unfair ridicule of the city, but when curious tourists and the media arrived and put Monterey on the map, the Chamber members changed their minds. While John and Carol were on a trip to Mexico, Otis sold the movie rights to *Tortilla Flat* for four thousand dollars.

Meanwhile, Steinbeck sold "The White Quail" to the *North American Review* and worked on his novel about labor organizers, *In Dubious Battle.* Otis convinced Covici to publish it in 1936. Its dramatic social protest themes caused immediate uproar on both the political left and right. In the spring of 1936, Steinbeck wrote *Of Mice and Men,* a title suggested by his friend Ricketts; Steinbeck structured this story about two migrants, Lennie and George, as a play in novel form. Published in February 1937, *Of Mice and Men* sold one hundred thousand copies, became an immediate best-seller, and was a Book-of-the-Month Club featured selection. Steinbeck, who liked to portray the image of the starving artist, wrote to Otis about his profits, "I shall never learn to conceive of money in larger quantities than two dollars. More than that has no conceptual meaning for me. . . . It will, [however], let me work without a starvation scare going on all the time. This may or may not be a good thing." As if strong book sales were not enough, playwright-director George S. Kaufman wanted to direct a stage version of *Of Mice and Men* as a fall production. Steinbeck converted the novel into a script, and the play won the New York Drama Critics' Circle Award for 1937. Parini describes Steinbeck's reaction to his sudden fame.

> He found himself in a bind that would become only too familiar. His growing reputation had turned him, suddenly, into a public person, but his shyness and his essential disbelief in publicity and "society" tugged him in the opposite direction. "He was never happy at parties," Elaine Steinbeck [his third wife] says. "Never in his life. And he always detested public events. He would much rather stay home and read, or write, or talk to friends. Publicity always depressed him."

DUST BOWL MIGRANTS

While Steinbeck was finishing the revisions of *Of Mice and Men*, the chief editor of the *San Francisco News*, George West, asked him to write a series of articles on migrant farm labor in California, particularly migrants who had fled the dust bowl of the Midwest during the depression. Steinbeck did field research by traveling from one migrant camp to another in an old bakery delivery truck, which he had equipped for camping, with Eric H. Thomsen, director in charge of management of the migrant camps in the region of the San Joaquin Valley. Steinbeck had seen the slum outside Salinas, called "Little Oklahoma," and the labor camps, called Hoovervilles, but the poverty and filth of the squatters' camps shocked him. He saw a three-year-old with a pot belly caused by malnutrition wearing only a burlap sack tied around his middle. He also saw the contrasting conditions of the government camps, which were clean and well run, and which offered inhabitants modest quarters. After completing the articles for the *San Francisco News*, he condensed the information for an article in the *Nation*. This research project gave Steinbeck an idea for a major book about migrant workers.

The Steinbecks went to New York to complete the script for *Of Mice and Men*. While in New York, Steinbeck's distaste for celebrity deepened. Now he was identified as a friend of the poor, and special interest groups increasingly turned to him for support and money. Feeling hounded, he and Carol bought a car and drove to Chicago to visit Steinbeck's Uncle Joe Hamilton. The main purpose of the auto trip, however, was to travel the route that the migrants took when they left the Oklahoma dust bowl and migrated to California. Benson describes Steinbeck's reaction to the suffering he saw:

> He wanted to lash out against the suffering and injustice that he had seen. As he wrote his agents sometime later, after coming back from another trip to the Valley, "Funny how mean and little books become in the face of such tragedies" [2/38]. He struggled for many months with the temptation to satirize and attack those who, through their greed and indifference, made such widespread suffering possible, and then he struggled with the sense that his subject was just too big, too emotionally overpowering, for him to handle. He wasn't able to write *The Grapes of Wrath* until he was able to contain his anger—and that took almost two years.

After the Steinbecks returned to California, they bought the fifty-acre ranch that Carol wanted. Uncomfortable with her husband's fame, she wanted a settled, quiet life with time to decorate the house, but Steinbeck wanted to work on his book about migrants. Their interests clashed, and tensions arose between them. Finally, during the summer of 1938, Steinbeck got control of his book about Oklahoma migrant workers, for which Carol supplied the title, *The Grapes of Wrath*, from a line in the lyrics of "The Battle Hymn of the Republic." He finished the manuscript in October 1938, and dedicated it to Carol and Tom Collins, the manager of the well-run government camps. By this time Covici was bankrupt and had gone to work for Viking Press, taking all of the Steinbeck works with him. Viking published *The Grapes of Wrath* just as Steinbeck had written it, though its editors had recommended changing the ending.

The Grapes of Wrath came out in March 1939, moved quickly to the top of the best-seller list and remained there well into 1940. This book, establishing Steinbeck as the country's preeminent serious novelist, won attention both as a literary work and as a political document. Most reviews praised the book, but many were confused by the end, when Rose of Sharon saves the life of an old man she does not know. Some critical readers found Steinbeck's language and realism shocking, but Steinbeck was particularly pleased when First Lady Eleanor Roosevelt toured the migrant camps and told the press that Steinbeck's book was an accurate portrayal.

FILMS, TRAVEL, AND THE WAR

Steinbeck and Carol often traveled to Hollywood as film studios bought the rights to his novels. Steinbeck became friends with Henry Fonda, who played Tom Joad in *The Grapes of Wrath*, and with Spencer Tracy, who starred in *The Red Pony*. *Of Mice and Men* was also produced as a feature film. Steinbeck grew to like Hollywood and the people and activity connected with filming, but Carol did not. On one such trip, tensions mounted between them, and Carol returned to the ranch. In her absence, John met Gwendolyn Conger, an attractive woman who wanted to be a singer and an actress.

During the decade of the forties, Steinbeck devoted his attention to travel and World War II, and his personal life remained unsettled. The decade began with a research trip with Ricketts in 1940 to the Sea of Cortez in Mexico. At Carol's insistence, she went along, hoping the trip would save their faltering marriage. On the voyage, Ricketts and Steinbeck discussed science, philosophy, and literature, and Stein-

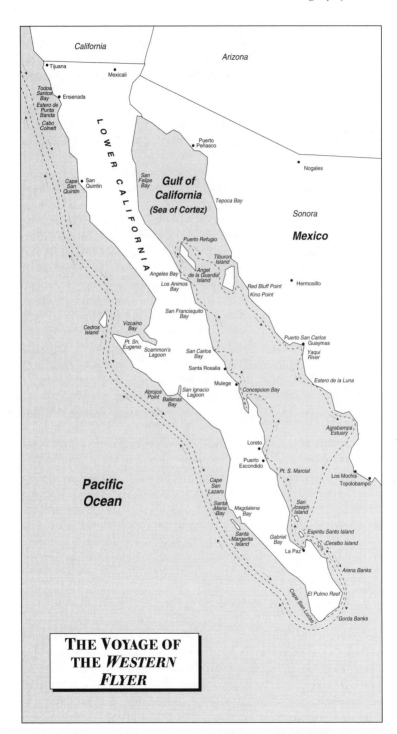

California

Arizona

Tijuana

Mexicali

Todos Santos Bay

Ensenada

Estero de Punta Banda

Cabo Colnett

Puerto Peñasco

Nogales

L O W E R   C A L I F O R N I A

San Felipe Bay

Cape San Quintin

San Quintin

Gulf of California

(Sea of Cortez)

Tepoca Bay

Sonora

Mexico

Puerto Refugio

Tiburon Island

Angel de la Guardia Island

Red Bluff Point

Kino Point

Hermosillo

Angeles Bay

Los Animos Bay

San Francisquito Bay

Vizcaino Bay

Cedros Island

Pt. Sn. Eugenio

Scammon's Lagoon

San Carlos Bay

Santa Rosalia

Mulege

Concepcion Bay

Puerto San Carlos

Guaymas

Yaqui River

Estero de la Luna

Abrojos Point

Ballenas Bay

San Ignacio Lagoon

Agrabampa Estuary

Loreto

Puerto Escondido

Pt. S. Marcial

Los Mochis

Topolobampo

Pacific Ocean

Cape San Lazaro

Santa Maria Bay

Magdalena Bay

San Joseph Island

Santa Margarita Island

Gabriel Bay

Espiritu Santo Island

Ceralbo Island

La Paz

Arena Banks

Cape San Lucas

El Pulmo Reef

Gorda Banks

THE VOYAGE OF THE *WESTERN* FLYER

beck kept a journal recording these conversations. At a stop at La Paz, Steinbeck heard a story about a boy and a giant pearl that formed the basis for his later book *The Pearl*. When they returned, Steinbeck learned that he had been awarded the Pulitzer Prize for *The Grapes of Wrath*. He also wrote the *Sea of Cortez: A Leisurely Journal of Travel and Research*, which he published with Ricketts as coauthor. The trip did not restore the Steinbecks' marriage, and Steinbeck began seeing Gwen Conger.

War occupied Steinbeck's attention off and on throughout the 1940s. He wrote *The Moon Is Down*, a story about Nazi invaders that could have taken place in any location, finishing the manuscript in November 1941, just before the Japanese invasion of Pearl Harbor in December. The book came out in February 1942, outselling *The Grapes of Wrath* in the first few weeks, and was produced as a play that opened in April. The war inspired Steinbeck to write scripts for propaganda films and to work as a war correspondent. In June 1943, he went to London as a correspondent for the New York *Herald-Tribune* and in August to North Africa to cover the invasion of Italy. After the war, Steinbeck and war photographer Robert Capa traveled to Russia for the *Herald-Tribune* to cover the effects of war on common people. Steinbeck developed these articles into a book entitled *A Russian Journal*.

BOOKS, SCRIPTS, AND FAILED MARRIAGES

Amid writing, traveling to locations for filmings, and moving between New York and California, Steinbeck's personal life was in upheaval. When he and Carol separated, she moved to New York, and Gwen Conger lived with Steinbeck. The divorce from Carol was final in March 1943, and John and Gwen were married. Gwen was discontent when Steinbeck made numerous trips, sometimes alone. To please her, Steinbeck tried moving back to California in 1944 and then back to New York. They had two sons: Thom, born in 1944, and John, born in 1946.

In addition to all of his trips and moves from one coast to the other, Steinbeck wrote several books during the decade. He worked on *Cannery Row* in 1944 after he and Gwen temporarily moved back to Monterey. The book focuses on the dockworkers he had met with Ricketts, and was published in 1945. In 1947, Steinbeck published *The Pearl*, the short novel he had developed from the story he had heard in La Paz; in it a pearl diver finds a very large pearl of great value, but he throws it back into the sea after his discovery causes nothing but trouble and, indirectly, the death of his son. *The Wayward Bus*, also published in 1947, is a symbolic story about people on a journey. *The Russian Journal* came out in 1948 and *Burning Bright* in 1950.

Steinbeck made many trips throughout the 1940s to work on films and plays. He went to Mexico City for the filming of *The Forgotten Village*, a semifictional documentary focusing on efforts to improve medical care in a Mexican village. He went to Hollywood for the filming of *Tortilla Flat*. In April 1945, he was back in Mexico City and Cuernavaca for the filming of *The Pearl*. Twice he worked on propaganda films for the American government. He wrote the scripts for *Bombs Away: The Story of a Bomber Team* and *Lifeboat*, a film he made with Alfred Hitchcock. In New York a musical play version of *Burning Bright*, Steinbeck's attempt to write a modern-day Everyman tale, closed after thirteen performances. He also worked on a film, *Viva Zapata!*, starring Marlon Brando, chronicling the story of Emiliano Zapata, a Mexican who led a revolt for agrarian reform.

Early in 1948, Steinbeck went to Salinas and Monterey to research a book about the valley. After he returned to New York in April, he had surgery for an accident injury, and a few days later his friend Ricketts was killed in a car accident. Ricketts's death was devastating to Steinbeck. His grief was compounded when Gwen accused him of overdependence on Ricketts: "Without him you are nothing. You will now be the failure you were before you met him, and I don't want to be married to a failure!" Gwen took the boys and went to Los Angeles, where her mother lived, and Steinbeck took a short trip to Mexico and returned to Pacific Grove. Their divorce followed shortly.

A SETTLED PERSONAL LIFE AND A CAREER IN DECLINE

During the 1950s, Steinbeck enjoyed a more settled personal life, but his writing career declined with each book he published. In 1949, Steinbeck met Elaine Scott, wife of the film star Zachary Scott, and when her divorce was final in 1950, she and Steinbeck married. Steinbeck's sons continued to live with him during the summer, and Elaine's daughter Waverly lived with them permanently. The family spent several summers on Nantucket Island near Cape Cod, until John and Elaine bought a house in Sag Harbor on Long Island, New York. Steinbeck and Elaine made two long trips to Europe,

one in 1952 and another to Paris in 1954. With Elaine, Steinbeck felt he had finally found the woman who was right for
him, and she was as happy as he.

In February 1951, shortly after his marriage to Elaine,
Steinbeck began work on the novel he had wanted to write
about the Salinas Valley. It was the saga of a family beginning
with his grandfather Samuel Hamilton. By April, he realized
that the story of one family was insufficient to carry his
theme, and he created a second family, hoping to fuse the
two. *East of Eden,* as he called it, became a novel of 250,000
words, covering a period from the Civil War to the end of
World War I. The editors at Viking recommended many cuts
and changes, all of which Steinbeck refused, and Viking published it in the fall of 1952. The book sold well, but the critics
were harsh, declaring that Steinbeck's creative talent was
nearly spent. Then he revised *Cannery Row* and gave it a new
title, *Sweet Thursday,* which was published in 1954. The critical reception was worse, openly claiming that Steinbeck had
lost his ability. But he did not give up. In the spring of 1956,
he experimented with a new form of novel, a fable set in
France about a man named Pippin. It was published in 1957
as *The Short Reign of Pippin IV, A Fabrication.*

Benson contends that much criticism of Steinbeck's work
was politically motivated: Reviewers praised his political lib-
eralism and social realism, but after *The Grapes of Wrath,*
when Steinbeck turned to new subjects, they were disap-
pointed that "he didn't write the same book over and over
again." Steinbeck usually took a philosophical view of published reviews, but not always, as Benson describes:

> There were times when a particularly snide or stupid review
> sent him into a tantrum. Like a wounded bull he would rage
> through house or apartment, stopping only to string together
> litanies of misbegotten lineage or promises of terrible re-
> venge. But just as often he agreed with negative assessments
> of his work—he was never satisfied with what he wrote—and
> in the long run what seemed most important to him was that
> he try different kinds of things, even if he had to acknowledge
> later that the attempt had failed.

STEINBECK'S LAST EFFORTS AND GREATEST HONOR

At the beginning of the 1960s, Steinbeck told Elaine that he
thought he should retire, but after that declaration, he hastily
wrote *The Winter of Our Discontent* and sent it to Covici, who
published it in June 1961. He had hurried to finish it because
he wanted to begin a camping trip around America with

Elaine's French poodle, Charley. He kept a log of his trip and, based on his notes, wrote *Travels with Charley in Search of America*, which was published in 1962 and received decent reviews as a travelogue. His greatest honor came in October 1962 with the announcement from Sweden that he had been awarded the Nobel Prize in literature. Only five other Americans had received this prize: Sinclair Lewis, Eugene O'Neill, Pearl Buck, William Faulkner, and Ernest Hemingway.

The announcement was met with widespread critical protest attacking the rationality of giving Steinbeck the award and proclaiming that the Nobel committee was out of touch with American writing. Hundreds of letters of congratulations poured in from around the world and from his friends, however, and Steinbeck personally answered each one. He and Elaine flew to Stockholm on December 8 and were honored by the Swedish government, Steinbeck's Swedish publisher, and by the U.S. embassy, which held a grand dinner in his honor. The next night he delivered a "simple, dignified, and inspiring" speech, according to Parini, who quotes the core of its message:

> ". . . Literature was not promulgated by a pale and emasculated critical priesthood singing their litanies in empty churches—nor is it a game for the cloistered elect, the tinhorn mendicants of low-calorie despair. Literature is as old as speech. It grew out of human need for it, and it has not changed except to become more needed. The skalds, the bards, the writers are not separate and exclusive."

> He ended with a plea for understanding and communication in the age of the atom bomb: "Man himself has become the greatest hazard and our only hope. So that today, Saint John the Apostle may well be paraphrased: In the end is the *word*, and the word is *man*, and the word is *with* man."

During the remainder of the 1960s, Steinbeck spent his energy on politics. He had been invited to John F. Kennedy's inauguration in January 1961. After Kennedy's assassination in 1963, Steinbeck became friends with Lyndon Johnson and spent many evenings at the White House. He went to Vietnam in 1967 to report on the war for *Newsday*, a Long Island newspaper. After his return, he wrote to Elizabeth Otis, "I have nothing I can or want to communicate—a dry-as-dust, worked out feeling." In the year that followed, he had back surgery, a stroke, and a series of heart attacks. Steinbeck died of a massive heart attack on December 20, 1968, and was buried in Salinas, California. He was sixty-six years old.

CHARACTERS AND PLOT

MAIN CHARACTERS

Billy Buck—Carl Tiflin's ranch hand, a skilled horseman who understands Jody and befriends him when his father is harsh and punitive.

Gitano—a former resident of the area who comes back in his old age seeking work on the ranch. When his request is refused, he heads into the mountains on Carl's old horse supposedly to die.

Grandfather—Jody's maternal grandfather.

Jess Taylor—neighbor and owner of Ridge Ranch.

Carl Tiflin—Jody's father.

Jody Tiflin—a young boy living on a ranch in the Salinas Valley in California.

Ruth Tiflin—Jody's mother.

PLOT

The Red Pony is a collection of four short stories unified by recurring characters, themes, images, and symbols. The stories, which chronicle four episodes in ten-year-old Jody Tiflin's young life, reveal his growing maturity as he encounters hope and disappointment.

"The Gift," the first story, opens by establishing the simple daily routines on the Tiflin ranch and the relationships among the characters. On the second day Jody's father presents his son with a red pony and tack he bought in Salinas. Jody and ranch hand Billy Buck inspect the new red saddle and discuss the training strategy for the colt, which Jody names Gabilan, meaning "hawk." Every morning Jody rises early to brush Gabilan and learns to calm him by massaging his ankles and talking reassuringly. For weeks Billy works with Jody, teaching him how to train the colt to accept a halter and bridle and how to walk, trot, gallop, and stop according to Jody's commands. Finally, in the late fall Jody trains the pony to accept a saddle, but though he is ready to put pressure on the stirrups, Jody must work with the horse before he can mount and ride it, which he aims to do on Thanksgiving.

Jody hopes for dry weather until after Thanksgiving to avoid landing in the mud when Gabilan inevitably bucks him off in his first tries in the saddle, but the cold winter rains arrive early. On a day that looks fair, Billy assures Jody that he can leave Gabilan out in the corral while he is in school; if rain comes, Billy tells him, he will put the pony into the barn. At noon the wind comes up and cold rain falls, but Billy, stranded at a neighboring ranch, is unable to tend to the pony. When Jody returns from school, Gabilan is cold and wet. By the next morning, the pony shows symptoms of sickness and becomes sicker as each day passes despite Billy Buck's guidance and Jody's care; by Friday Billy realizes the horse has sprangles, an infectious disease of horses characterized by nasal inflammation and abscesses in the mouth.

During the weekend, Jody stays day and night in the stall. Billy has to cut open the sac under the horse's jaw to drain the pus; during the following night when Jody awakens to find the barn door blown open and the pony gone, he takes a lantern and leads him back in. On Sunday Gabilan struggles for breath; to give the pony air, Billy slits a small hole in the pony's windpipe, and Jody and Billy watch the pony all day to see that the hole stays open. The next morning, Jody awakens at daylight, finds the door blown open again, and the pony gone; he follows Gabilan's tracks to the brush line, where he sees the buzzards circling the horse waiting for him to die. Jody manages to grab a buzzard perched on his pony and in his frustration and anger crushes the buzzard's skull after the pony dies. Billy and Carl arrive. Carl reminds Jody that taking his frustration out on the buzzard isn't appropriate; Billy turns on his boss and carries Jody home.

At the beginning of the second story, "The Great Mountains," Jody is involved in a series of small cruel acts. He throws rocks to break the swallow nests plastered against the ceiling boards in the barn. He sets a rat trap knowing that Doubletree Mutt will spring it and get snapped on the nose, and then he throws rocks at the dog. After he kills a bird with his slingshot and cuts it up, he feels ashamed and goes to the brush line where a mossy tub was placed to catch spring water from a simple pipe. Lying in the green grass by the tub, Jody watches the clouds floating over the mountains and wonders what lies beyond the brown rocky mountains to the west and why the mountains to the east are green and populated with ranches. He recalls a conversation with his father when he had asked what lies beyond the brown mountains; his father told him that more mountains lie beyond, and discouraged his curiosity.

Turning his attention to the green mountains behind him, Jody spots an old man walking toward his house, and Jody runs to meet him. He is Gitano, a paisano, or peasant, who had lived in a nearby dobe (adobe) years ago and is now coming back in his old age to stay and work. Carl tells him he cannot work, but he can stay for dinner and sleep in the bunkhouse until morning. Showing Gitano to the bunkhouse gives Jody an opportunity to question him about the mountains. Though Gitano worked in Salinas Valley, he had gone into the mountains with his father once as a boy, but had never wanted to return. With Jody's persistence, he finally explains that the mountains are a quiet place of peace. To Jody, Gitano is as mysterious as the mountains.

The old man and the young boy go to the barnyard to look at the stock. Jody tells Gitano about Old Easter, the first horse his father bought thirty years ago, and Gitano responds that the horse is too old to work, that he just eats and will soon die. Billy and Carl stroll up to the fence. Carl in his hard way says that shooting Old Easter would put him out of the misery brought on by rheumatism and bad teeth, but Billy insists that a horse has a right to rest after long years of work. Carl draws an obvious parallel between Gitano and Old Easter, implying that both are old and useless; Jody tries to soften the remark as his father's way of joking.

After dinner Jody slips away from the family and visits Gitano in the bunkhouse, where he finds him polishing a rapier with a beautiful hand-carved handle. Jody questions him until Gitano says he got it from his father but knows nothing more about it. He wraps the rapier in the deerskin and sends Jody away. In the morning Gitano is gone, but his sack of clothes remains in the bunkhouse. Standing on the porch, Carl notices that Old Easter has not come down for water and figures he must have died during the night. Later that morning a neighboring rancher, Jess Taylor, arrives with the news that early in the morning he saw an old man on Easter riding into the mountains, using only a rope for a bridle and carrying something, a gun perhaps, across his lap. Hearing this, Jody goes to the water tub and sees a black speck crawling up a distant ridge. He lies on the grass by the tub wondering, his arms crossed over his eyes; he feels a great longing, and he is "full of a nameless sorrow."

The third story, "The Promise," opens in the spring. The horses romp in the pasture and the sheep and calves jump and play. Jody too is filled with spring energy, pretends he drums for a regiment on the way home from school, and fills his empty lunch pail with toads and insects. After a snack in the kitchen, his mother informs him his father wants to see him, news that makes Jody fear trouble. He is surprised when his father offers him the next colt of his mare Nellie if he promises to work off the breeding fee and to tend Nellie until the colt is born.

Jody takes Nellie up the hills to Jess Taylor's ranch to be bred to Taylor's stallion. Just as they turn up the drive, Jody hears a stallion's whistling scream and wood splintering. Nellie rears and whinnies, and when she comes at Jody with bared teeth, he drops the rope and runs into the brush. Again the stallion screams and again Nellie answers just as the stallion appears trailing a broken rope. The horses fight briefly until Nellie's mood changes and she rubs gently against the stallion. Jess Taylor rides up, puts Jody on his horse behind him, and the two wait while Nellie is bred. Jody pays the five-dollar breeding fee, and Jody takes a docile Nellie back home.

Jody now has nearly a year to wait for Nellie's colt to be born. He does his regular chicken-feeding chores responsibly and through the spring and summer learns to drive a hay rake, help bale hay, and milk a cow, new chores Carl adds at regular intervals. Jody goes to see Nellie every day, but after three months he can see no change in her. Billy assures him that the colt is developing even though no sign will be noticeable for several months. They discuss the differences between stallions and mares and how the birthing will go. Jody goes often to the green tub, where the water trickles from the iron pipe now grown rusty; the patch of green grass and the sound of the water soothe him when he has been punished and calm him when he feels mean and impatient. During his long wait, he has dreams in which he rides his black horse.

The first signs that there will indeed be a colt come in the fall. Ruth Tiflin teaches Jody to make the warm mash Nellie needs every morning, and Nellie grows quieter and friendlier. Winter comes and Christmas passes, and Jody spends all his spare time with Nellie enjoying the movements he feels when he touches her belly. Carl appears at the stall one day and tells Jody he has done a good job, the most praise and warmth he is able to offer his son. When Nellie's due date in January passes, Jody worries, and he pesters Billy for reassurance. On the second of February he awakens from a dream crying, slips on his clothes, and goes to the barn in bare feet. There he finds Nellie standing and swaying. Billy, sleeping in the hay, hears Jody and sends him back to bed so as not to bother the horse. But Jody has time only to shut his eyes when he feels Billy's hand urging him to come.

In the barn Nellie's body shakes with repeated spasms, but nothing happens, and Billy knows something is wrong. Using his hand to try to help Nellie, he realizes that the colt is turned wrong, he cannot turn it, and it cannot come out. Billy makes a quick hard decision and picks up the horseshoe hammer. He tells Jody to go outside, but Jody stands frozen. Billy walks to Nellie's head and tells Jody to turn his head. Jody hears the heavy hammer pound Nellie's forehead and crush her skull. The horse falls, quivers, and goes silent. With his big pocketknife Billy saws and rips the tough horsehide until he has made a long opening. Using both hands, he digs out the white sac holding the colt and uses his teeth to tear a hole. A little black head appears, and takes one gurgling breath after another until breath comes evenly. Billy cuts the cord, picks up the colt, and lays it in the straw at Jody's feet. Billy sends Jody to the house for warm water so that he can wash and dry the baby as its mother would have done.

The fourth story, "The Leader of the People," opens as Billy and Jody rake up a used haystack. Jody wants to scare out the mice for the dogs to chase, but Billy warns him to get his father's permission, knowing Carl likes to control everything on the ranch. Carl comes riding down the drive carrying a white letter in his hand. In the house Jody listens to his mother read the letter, from her father, who writes that he will arrive on Saturday. Carl complains because he hates listening to this old man repeat the same stories about leading a band of pioneers across the plains. Since this is already Saturday, Jody sets out to meet his grandfather and sees in the distance a cart pulled by a bay horse. The two ride to the ranch making small talk and plans to hunt mice the next day. On arrival mother, father, and Billy gather to greet the old man. At dinner Grandfather tells the same stories he has told dozens of times about finding food and fending off an Indian attack. Only Jody is interested and urges his grandfather on.

In the morning before Grandfather comes in to breakfast, Carl complains loudly about the old man's living in the past; that time is done, he says, and nobody wants to hear about it; he should just forget it. The old man opens the door, and Carl asks him if he has overheard him. Embarrassed, Carl says he did not mean what he said and apologizes. Grandfather assures him that he is not angry and that perhaps Carl is right. Despite Grandfather's gracious response, Carl gets up from the table and Billy follows, leaving Grandfather and Jody alone. Jody urges Grandfather to join him in hunting mice, but he declines and chooses to sit in the sun by himself. Jody tries the hunt alone, but discovers he has no enthusiasm for the game. Instead, he returns, asks Grandfather for more stories; the old man's last story concludes that it was the moving and the "westering" that were important and now that is all done because there is no place left to go. Grandfather wipes his eyes and contemplates his hands folded over his knees. Jody feels sad and offers to make lemonade for him. In the kitchen his mother gets down the squeezer and two lemons.

CHAPTER 1

Major Themes in *The Red Pony*

The Importance of the Salinas Valley Setting

Freeman Champney

Freeman Champney emphasizes that understanding Steinbeck's work necessitates knowing the Salinas Valley where Steinbeck was raised. Champney describes the valley's lush beauty and its rocky barren features as well as the harsh business practices of the prominent ranching and farming industries. Active in university and commercial publishing work, Freeman Champney was a founding editor of the *Antioch Review*. He has published *Art and Glory: The Story of Elbert Hubbard.*

Most of the critics . . . have discussed Steinbeck's books with little or no knowledge of the country in which he grew up and which he writes about. Even a casual direct contact with this country and its people suggests that this background is the most important thing to know about Steinbeck and that it explains much of his writing better than any amount of remote analysis. . . .

The Salinas Valley roughly parallels the coast, thirty miles or so inland, for most of its length of about a hundred and twenty miles. It is one of the smaller of California's central valleys, which run up and down the state between mountain ranges. The enclosing hills have the steep slopes and the barren, rounded crests which have evoked so many anatomical comparisons. During much of the year they are brown and dry, turning green during the rainy winter. The river, the highway, and the Southern Pacific Railroad chase each other down the valley floor. The river itself, like most California rivers, is normally sandy, brush-choked, and nearly dry but carries a great volume of floodwater when the big rains come. At the lower end of the valley the flat bottomland is cut into great fields of lettuce, broccoli, alfalfa,

Excerpted from Freeman Champney, "John Steinbeck, Californian," *The Antioch Review*, vol. 8, no. 3. Copyright © 1947 by The Antioch Review, Inc. Reprinted by permission of the editors.

sugar beets, and other truck crops. Cattle are raised on the slopes of the hills. Salinas (where Steinbeck was born and raised) is about ten miles inland from the river's mouth in Monterey Bay. It is the county seat and the trading and shipping center for the lower part of the valley. It looks a little more metropolitan than the raw valley towns but not much more.

MAJOR OCCUPATIONS IN SALINAS

Cattle-raising has been a valley occupation since the days of the missions but the intensive cultivation of vegetables—especially lettuce, which takes up more than 50,000 acres—has outranked it in importance for some time. But the nostalgic glamor of the cowhand days is clung to. You see fifty lean men in sombreros, tight jeans, and riding boots for every visible horse. Once a year Salinas stages "California's Biggest Rodeo" and cashes in handsomely on its nostalgia.

Lettuce, however, is the big industry of the valley, and its growing, packing, and shipping follow the highly capitalized pattern of California agriculture that [historian] Carey McWilliams has accurately called "Factories in the Field." In 1936 a strike by lettuce packing shed workers was crushed at a cost of around a quarter of a million dollars. Civil liberties, local government, and normal judicial processes were all suspended during the strike and Salinas was governed by a general staff directed by the Associated Farmers and the big lettuce growers and shippers. The local police were bossed by a reserve army officer imported for the job, and at the height of the strike all male residents of Salinas between 18 and 45 were mobilized under penalty of arrest, were deputized and armed. Beatings, tear gas attacks, wholesale arrests, threats to lynch San Francisco newspapermen if they didn't leave town, and machine guns and barbed wire all figured in the month-long struggle which finally broke the strike and destroyed the union.

So much for John Steinbeck's birthplace, where he lived his first nineteen years. From Salinas it is about fifteen miles through a pass in the Santa Lucia Range to the Monterey Peninsula. This fantastic area contains some of the most picturesque country in the world and an assortment of humanity almost as bizarre and much less permanent. Monterey itself is tough and raucous. Its harbor shelters the purse seiners of the sardine fleet. . . .

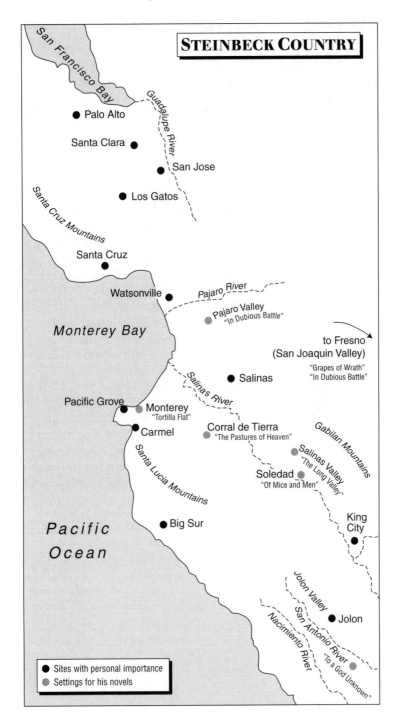

STEINBECK COUNTRY

San Francisco Bay

Guadalupe River

● Palo Alto

Santa Clara ●

● San Jose

● Los Gatos

Santa Cruz Mountains

Santa Cruz
●

Watsonville ●

Pajaro River

Pajaro Valley
"In Dubious Battle"

Monterey Bay

to Fresno
(San Joaquin Valley)

"Grapes of Wrath"
"In Dubious Battle"

Salinas River

● Salinas

Pacific Grove ●

Monterey
"Tortilla Flat"

Corral de Tierra
"The Pastures of Heaven"

Gabilan Mountains

Carmel

Salinas Valley
"The Long Valley"

Santa Lucia Mountains

Soledad ●
"Of Mice and Men"

Pacific

● Big Sur

King
City
●

Ocean

Jolon Valley

San Antonio River

"To a God Unknown"

● Jolon

Nacimiento River

● Sites with personal importance
● Settings for his novels

RICH OWNERS DOMINATE POOR WORKERS

The cultural climate of the Salinas Valley is typical of California agriculture. A tradition of personal individualism goes along with a strongly collectivized economy. As Carey McWilliams has pointed out, the great California valleys show few resemblances to traditional American rural life. The "school-house on the hilltop, the comfortable homes, the compact and easy indolence of the countryside" are noticeably absent. Instead there are the vast orchards, vineyards, and ranches, meticulously tended, irrigated, and smudged but showing little close functional connection with human life. They are (most of them) really farm factories, and their financing and cultivation, and the marketing of their output, have become highly collectivized activities, managed by and for the great owners and packers, the banks, and the utilities. As in most big business, ownership and management are usually sharply separated. The exploitation of labor has exceeded anything known in Western civilization since the early mill towns of England. The operators of this paradise have usually been able to use or usurp the sovereign powers of local or state government whenever necessary to wipe out a threat to their absolutism.

Economically, socially, and culturally it has been an ugly state of affairs. In its extremes of wealth and destitution, in the absence or impotence of any middle group representing the public interest, and in the domination of the organs of civil life by irresponsible private greed, it has been one of the few areas of American life that has closely approximated the Marxian predictions about capitalist society.

Charles Darwin and Steinbeck's Ideal Hero

Brian E. Railsback

Brian E. Railsback argues that evolutionary biologist Charles Darwin and John Steinbeck look on humanity with a similar scientific view and agree on the traits that most set humans apart from other creatures. Though Billy Buck, the farmhand in *The Red Pony*, fails to measure up as an ideal man, he comes close. Brian E. Railsback, who teaches writing at Western Carolina University, Cullowhee, North Carolina, is the author of scholarly articles published in *San Jose Studies* and the *Steinbeck Quarterly*.

So we are animals, part of the same whole that is the aggregate of all life on Earth. But surely we are something more, and isolating that "more" has been the business of theologians and philosophers ever since we evolved enough to consider the problem. [The biologist Charles] Darwin and Steinbeck, from their scientific view of the human as a species, conclude what the difference is, or may some day be. The problem involves nothing less than defining humanity. Strikers and soldiers may fight with the brutality of beasts, men and women may love with the ferocity of animals, but there are also those with a wider vision. Monkeys never negotiated a peace, designed a machine, nor estimated the size of a galaxy. This chapter examines how Darwin and Steinbeck extract the "more," the human, from the "less" in *Homo sapiens*.

STEINBECK AND DARWIN AGREE ON THE HIGHEST HUMAN QUALITIES

We can trace in Steinbeck's work a quest to find what qualities in a human are different from those of a beast. In this sense, Steinbeck's fiction follows a line of development, a kind of evolution in itself, in which the author creates a

Excerpted from Brian E. Railsback, *Parallel Expeditions: Charles Darwin and the Art of John Steinbeck* (Moscow, ID: University of Idaho Press, 1995). Reprinted with permission.

hero, exposes a flaw, and tears the hero down. Eventually he arrives at a hero who resists destruction, who proves a worthy example of what, in Steinbeck's view, a good human being should be. As Steinbeck and Darwin follow the same course, how they define the human in humanity is remarkably similar. Indeed, the "Doc" characters[1] and Charles Darwin share many traits. This bright view of humanity came gradually for Steinbeck, a product of the kind of developing process the novelist describes in his response to *Steinbeck and His Critics:* "It is always astonishing to read a critique of one's work. In my own case, it didn't come out that way but emerged little by little, staggering and struggling . . . then, after the fact—long after—a pattern is discernible, a clear and fairly consistent pattern" ("Postscript" 307).

Before defining Steinbeck's conception of the hero, or the humane person, we should examine how Darwin defined a person at the highest level of civilized development. The naturalist's writing, particularly his *Autobiography, The Descent of Man,* and various letters, presents a reasonable picture of those qualities Darwin would have found of the highest order in humanity. Not surprisingly, these characteristics make up much of Darwin's own nature as he and others perceived it.

Darwin wants to see things in a most unprejudiced way, to observe without preconception, and to do so requires a mixture of bravery and humility. Bravery asserts a new idea that runs counter to most popular scientific and theological concepts; humility presents it in the truest way, without distortions caused by an eye toward fame. Observation and inductive thinking are crucial to the naturalist's method. . . .

The inductive method of thinking led to Darwin's greatness, which was recognized in his lifetime but is not a product of some conscious desire to become famous. Darwin searched for truth in nature, and fame was a by-product rather than a goal: "I did not care much about the general public. I do not mean to say that a favourable review or a large sale of my books did not please me greatly, but the pleasure was a fleeting one, and I am sure that I have never turned one inch out of my course to gain fame" (*Autobiography* 52). In fact, Darwin tried to duck fame and controversy; he wanted to get on quietly with his work and proba-

---

1. characters named Doc appear in several of Steinbeck's works; they embody the traits Steinbeck considers good—they are strong, humble, compassionate, inductive seekers of truth and knowledge—men in touch with the whole.

bly knew that any inflation of ego would blur his ability to observe and think inductively. As we know from [Jackson J.] Benson's biography of Steinbeck, *The True Adventures of John Steinbeck, Writer,* and the author's own comments in his *Grapes of Wrath* journal, (*Working Days*), Steinbeck also dreaded fame. He even feared that winning the Nobel Prize might hurt his work (which it did).

The personal humility of both men can clearly be seen by the way they accepted the greatest honors ever presented to them. In 1864 Darwin received England's highest scientific honor: the Copley Medal of the Royal Society. As his son Francis explains, Darwin felt too ill to accept the award personally, and the naturalist's response to the honor illustrates his view of fame: "The Copley, being open to all sciences and all the world, is reckoned a great honour; but excepting from several kind letters, such things make little difference to me" (*Autobiography* 274). Benson has carefully recorded Steinbeck's reaction to receiving the Nobel Prize; the author was ecstatic, but at a press conference his humility helped feed critics who were hungry to deride him. Benson describes what happened after a reporter asked Steinbeck if he really deserved the prize: "If he had a little more ego, he would have lost his temper; if he had been more of a politician, he would have said that was for the committee to decide; but being John Steinbeck, he looked straight into the eyes of the reporter and said, 'Frankly, no'" (*True Adventures* 915).

Charles Darwin praised observation and induction and could submerge ego enough to accept what appeared to him as truth. The "is" thinking of Steinbeck and Ricketts[2] works in precisely the same way. To each of them, this cognitive process, requiring absolute avoidance of prejudice in order to be most successful, represents a superior way of ascertaining truth. Although such a way of thinking represents a more advanced mind, both Darwin and Steinbeck focus on a single quality that separates the beast from the humane person: sympathy.

SYMPATHY DISTINGUISHES THE HUMANE PERSON

The naturalist reveres sympathy and estimates other individuals and humanity in general by this quality; he finds its cousins, empathy, compassion, and cooperation, to be essential components of the highly developed human being.

2. Ed Ricketts, a marine biologist, was a close friend of Steinbeck's and discussed biology with him.

Writing of [geologist Sir Charles] Lyell in his autobiography, he lauds him with the observation that "one of his chief characteristics was his sympathy with the work of others" (*Autobiography* 33). In recounting his winning of the Royal Medal in 1853, Darwin typically plays down the award but seizes on the warmth of a congratulatory letter from J.D. Hooker (another Darwin defender): "Believe me, I shall not soon forget the pleasure of your letter. Such hearty, affectionate sympathy is worth more than all the medals that ever were or will be coined" (*Autobiography* 172). Writing of his father, whom Darwin admired highly, he calls him "the most perfect sympathiser" (*Autobiography* 91).

His own admiration for this quality finds its way into *The Descent of Man*. Sympathy is chief among the "moral qualities" which distinguish humans from animals. Morality arises from social instincts, which we share with other animals. "These instincts are highly complex, and in the case of the lower animals give special tendencies towards certain definite actions," Darwin writes, "but the more important elements are love, and the distinct emotion of sympathy." He also notes that these social instincts "are highly beneficial to the species," as mutual cooperation facilitates survival, and "have in all probability been acquired through natural selection." Further, he calls sympathy "one of the most important elements of the social instincts," crucial to the survival of a species as it develops cooperation. In the last line of the book, he writes that "sympathy which feels for the most debased" is foremost among the human's "noble qualities." Darwin uses sympathy as Steinbeck uses the term *simpatico* in *The Log:* it promotes active cooperation. Both Darwin and Steinbeck might naturally regard sympathy as important for it requires one to see and feel beyond the self and is an emotion that works in tandem with their method of thinking.

SYMPATHY AND REASON LEAD TO TRUTH

Sympathetic emotions and inductive reasoning will likely defy prejudice and ultimately bring one closer to truth. For Darwin the goal is to define what is true; for Steinbeck the goal is to depict the truth. The whole notion of "what actually 'is'" involves moving beyond personal and cultural preconceptions. An inductive thinker who observes without bias, submerges ego, and possesses sympathy stands the best chance of knowing truth. Above all else, the work of

Darwin and Steinbeck represents an effort to present, with the aid of science, a truthful view of our place in the world— no matter whose prejudices might be destroyed as a consequence.

The qualities that Darwin most admires define Steinbeck's hero, the kind of human being that the author spent nearly a lifetime searching for and portraying. The most noble of Steinbeck's characters think inductively, accept the "is" about themselves and the world, and extend beyond self to become the quintessence of sympathy, compassion, and cooperation. These people, exceptionally honest with themselves and others, are the ones who will resist the beast and push humanity another step forward. In times of struggle, they are the cooperators, and they are the ones who will endure. . . .

BILLY BUCK APPROACHES THE IDEAL

By 1938, Steinbeck comes close to his ideal with Billy Buck of the stories in *The Red Pony* (first published in *The Long Valley* and then as a separate book in 1945). Buck has strength, wisdom, purpose, and great compassion. He lacks the greed of Morgan, the monomania of Wayne, and the aimlessness of the paisanos.[3] Buck is as essential a part of the Tiflin ranch as he is of Jody Tiflin's life. Carl, Jody's father, has a certain degree of wisdom, but his compassion is choked off by his crushing pragmatism. Buck knows how a boy feels. However, Buck suffers from a flaw similar to Joseph Wayne's: he thinks he knows nature well enough to make it fit his plans and expectations. While the paisanos, in their easy acceptance of things, know the best-laid plans will go awry, Buck must endure some painful lessons in nature's school. To his credit, Buck does his best to learn, but his pride and his love for Jody get in the way. *The Red Pony*, like so much of Steinbeck's work, is an object lesson of our place in the world: no one dominates the natural scheme and no one can make promises against the greater machinations of the universe.

Buck is a strong, good ranch hand and has a degree of humility; he knows to wait on the steps rather than be the first in the dining room for breakfast, understanding his station as a hand. Yet Buck prides himself as an infallible teacher in

3. Morgan of *Cup of Gold*, Wayne of *To a God Unknown*, and the paisanos (peasants) of *Tortilla Flat.*

the natural school; in the first pages of *The Red Pony* he instructs Jody on things from egg yolks to horse care. Jody, a wide-open boy eager to learn, accepts the ranch hand's word as perfect. Buck is in touch with nature, even explaining to Jody the need to converse with a horse to ease its fears. Such communion with nature indicates that, in Steinbeck's world, this is a good character—a man in tune with the whole.

Buck has set himself up in his own and Jody's eyes as an expert on nature: "Buck wasn't wrong about many things. He couldn't be." That "couldn't be" suggests the trap Buck has set for himself, and the problems arising from the red pony, Gabilan, soon prove that even Buck cannot predict nature. He leaves the horse out in a storm, having erroneously assumed the weather would be fair. Although he predicts the horse will be all right, it becomes gravely ill and, despite all his efforts to save it, the red pony dies horribly. Jody strikes back at nature, killing one of the buzzards feasting on the dead pony—the act has little effect, however, for the bird's "red fearless eyes still looked at him, impersonal and unafraid and detached." The boy and Buck know the gesture is useless, and they learn a lesson about promises, plans, and the greater processes of nature. The lesson does not hold.

Later in *The Red Pony*, in the chapter entitled "The Promise," Buck falls into the same trap as before. Trying to recover the position he has lost in Jody's eyes, he wants desperately to deliver Nellie's colt (which Tiflin has said will be Jody's). After warning that he cannot promise Jody anything, Buck soon feels proud again, telling Jody: "I'll see you get a good colt. I'll start you right." To make his promise right, Buck has to kill and dismember Nellie to retrieve the colt from an impossible breach position. As [critic] Robert H. Woodward has shown, Buck becomes obsessed with trying to keep his promise to Jody. To fulfill the promise, nature has called for a bloody sacrifice, and neither the angered Buck nor the appalled Jody feel good about it.

Buck has made mistakes, but unlike Wayne, he is not destroyed by them. In the final chapter, "The Leader of the People," Jody eagerly plots the destruction of some mice, observing that they have no idea what will soon happen to them. "No, nor you either," Buck tells Jody, "nor me, nor anyone." (In the original manuscript, Steinbeck crossed out a passage that equated the mice with people, personifying them as "mother mice, the caucuses of political mice, the gossiping cliques of social mice, the young fairy mice, all would go to the death hunted down by . . . Jody—Fate.") Just as Buck knows his place among men as a ranch hand, he must learn his place in nature as a human being. He has the wisdom and humility to accept the lesson and, unlike the paisanos, he can do something useful with it by passing it on to Jody.

Group Theory in "The Leader of the People"

Richard Astro

Richard Astro explains Steinbeck's phalanx theory;
that is, his ideas about the relationship of individuals
to the groups to which they belong. With his friend
Edward F. Ricketts, Steinbeck studied group behavior
of animals and fish and then compared it to human
behavior. Astro illustrates Steinbeck's theory by ap-
plying it to "The Leader of the People." Richard Astro, who has taught at Oregon State University, is the
coeditor of *Steinbeck: The Man and His Work* (with
Tetsumaro Hayashi) and of *Steinbeck and the Sea*
(with Joel Hedgpeth).

There are some striking differences and similarities in Ricketts'[1] and Steinbeck's ideas concerning the relationship between the individual man and the groups or societies in
which he functions. Both were interested in the way animals
behave within groups, and they wrestled with the possibility
that men, like many species of lower animals, may be nothing apart from the groups to which they belong and from
which they draw much of their identity. And yet, just as the
two agreed that there are fundamental differences between
men and animals, so they shared in large measure some
very definite ideas about the importance of the individual
man as opposed to the individual marine organism.

Ricketts was vitally interested in what happens to the individual man in collective movements, and he notes in a
journal kept during his stay at the Monterey Presidio that the
forced patterns imposed upon soldiers may result in benefits
to those soldiers which outweigh their individual loss of
freedom:

1. Edward F. Ricketts, a marine biologist, was Steinbeck's closest personal friend and
intellectual companion for nearly two decades. Both men were interested in the patterns of schools of fish in tide pools. That interest led them to think about the behavior of humans in groups.

Excerpted from Richard Astro, *John Steinbeck and Edward F. Ricketts: The Shaping of
a Novelist* (Minneapolis: University of Minnesota Press, 1973). Reprinted with permission.

What they give up is practically everything they have had or striven for, sometimes even life itself. Often freedom. What they get is in direct ratio to what they give up, because the army forges its deep bond of companionship between men who have lost everything but each other and (deeply, dedicatedly) themselves. And just as many a wife or husband has a greatness in human relation larger than they are themselves, so a rather insignificant soldier can have thrust upon him a great mantle of mass-love. Merely by being a member of a group—a forced member. They don't know it, many are insensitive, not conscious. But they are in it and of it. They are it.

By and large, however, though the highly individualistic Ricketts acknowledges that there are human as well as tide pool societies in which "the individual serves the state, chiefly as a unit or cog in the supra-personal social organization that is the colony," he espouses a clear preference for another kind of society, which is "based on the democratic principle in which the state serves the individual." In his Sea of Cortez journal, Ricketts comments on a group of Japanese fishermen who, at the bidding of the collective Japanese mind, are depleting the shrimp resources of Guaymas while the Mexican Department of Marine watches in helpless dismay. He observes that "there again is the conflict of nations, of ideologies, of two conflicting organisms. And the units in those organisms are themselves good people, people you'd like to know, like the kind young Jap captain."

Similarly, in his "Anti-script" to *The Forgotten Village*, Ricketts wonders why group movements are so inflexible and summarily concludes that whereas the individual, "by intent, discipline and skill" can "walk the knife edge" and channel his "life energy" as he sees fit, "the group, having started in one direction, tends to develop along those lines until it exhibits the law of diminishing returns, or until it contacts powerful opposite influence."

STEINBECK'S THOUGHTS ON INDIVIDUALS IN GROUPS

Steinbeck's interest in the relationship between the individual and the group plays a crucial thematic role in much of his fiction and is somewhat more complex and sophisticated than that demonstrated by Ricketts. And yet a cursory reading of the criticism of his work reveals that he has been much maligned for being unwilling or unable to distinguish the individual as a distinct "unit," apart from the interest groups in which he functions. Steinbeck has been condemned for an alleged commitment to collectivism in which [, according to critic John S. Kennedy,] "life's fullness is found only in the group and never in the individual."

Those who decry Steinbeck's failure to recognize the individual do not seem to understand that the novelist denies that man's participation in a group necessarily negates his individuality. This can happen, of course, and Steinbeck's characters often victimize themselves by selling their souls to collective bodies. The crucial point, however, is that their capitulation to the group is thematically purposeful on Steinbeck's part, and the novelist demonstrates how each character who forfeits his individuality violates his own integrity.

As a student of modern mass movements, Steinbeck examined closely the question whether man can have any individuality apart from the group in which he functions. Similarly, he studied the origin and direction of groups to ascertain why some groups enable human freedom while others destroy it. When, through Ricketts, he learned [ecological theorist W.C.] Allee's ideas about the automatic behavioral patterns of animal aggregations, Steinbeck wrote a two-page paper on the subject of group behavior, "Argument of Phalanx." According to Richard Albee, to whom Steinbeck gave the paper, it was written in Pacific Grove sometime between 1934 and 1936 and was titled after the use of the term *phalanx*[2] for the battle formations of the Roman legions. . . .

STEINBECK'S "ARGUMENT OF PHALANX"

"We have thought of mankind always in terms of individual men," Steinbeck writes in "Argument of Phalanx."

> We have tried to study men and movements of men by minute investigation of individual men-units. We might as reasonably try to understand the nature of a man by investigating the cells of his body. Perhaps if we observe the phalanx, knowing it is a new individual, not to be confused with the units which compose it, if we look back at the things it has done in an attempt to correlate and analyse its habits under various stimuli, we may in time come to know something of the phalanx, of its nature, of its drive and its ends, we may even be able to direct its movements where now we have only great numbers of meaningless, unrelated and destructive phenomena.

Confirming [William Emerson Ritter's] doctrine of organismal biology that "the organism in its totality is as essential

2. an array of soldiers in close order

to an explanation of its elements as its elements are to an explanation of the organism," Steinbeck insists that men must be regarded as "units in the greater beast, the phalanx."

> Within the body of a man are units, cells, some highly specialized and some coordinate, which have their natures and their lives, which die and are replaced, which suffer and are killed. In their billions they make up man, the new individual. But man is more than the total of his cells, and his nature is not that of the sum of all his cells. He has a nature now new and strange to his cells.
>
> Man is a unit of the greater beast, the phalanx. The phalanx has pains, desires, hungers, and strivings as different from those of the unit man's as man's are different from the unit cells.

Just as Ricketts suggests that individual soldiers may not comprehend fully what happens to them in the military "whole," Steinbeck observes that the emotions of the phalanx are "foreign and incomprehensible to unit-man." And yet, quoting perhaps the most crucial section of the phalanx paper, "Within each unit-man, deep in him, in his subconscious, there is a keying device with which he may become part of the phalanx."

> Once he is part of a moving phalanx, his nature changes, his habits and his desires. When the phalanx is in motion, it controls its unit-men with an iron discipline. In phalanx need there can be change of birth rate of the units, of the stature, complexion, color, constitution of the unit. Phalanx resistance to circumstance is far greater than individual man's resistance. Once a man has become a unit in a phalanx in motion, he is capable of prodigies of endurance of thought or of emotion such as would be unthinkable were he acting as individual man. . . . All life forms from protozoa to antelopes and lions, from crabs to lemmings form and are a part of phalanxes, but the phalanx of which the units are men, are more complex, more variable and powerful than any other.

. . . Much of Steinbeck's thinking about the group-man grew from his interest in the aggregational patterns of life in the tide pools, and he often draws comparisons between the group-man and the group-animal for purposes of analogy. Never, however, does he say they are synonymous. The *idea* of the group-man is certainly analogous to the *idea* of the group-fish, but, and here Steinbeck moves beyond Ricketts, the purposive, mind-directed objectives of the group-man (in contrast to the chiefly regulative and adaptive behavior of the group-fish) are distinctly human and, in the best of groups, enhance and elevate the self rather than destroy it. . . .

A HUMAN SPIRIT IN GRANDFATHER'S WESTERING

In "The Leader of the People," originally published as a short story in *The Long Valley*, but now the final section of *The Red Pony*, Grandfather's participation in the movement called westering can in no way be equated with the actions of the group-fish.

> We carried life out here and set it down the way those ants carry eggs. And I was the leader. The westering was as big as God, and the slow steps that made the movement piled up and piled up until the continent was crossed.

True, westering was, as Grandfather says, "a whole bunch of people made into one big crawling beast," but it was a uniquely human beast, an energetic force composed of individual men finding personal meaning and direction through joint participation in a concerted effort ("'Every man wanted something for himself, but the big beast that was all of them wanted only westering.'"). Westering, unlike animal migration, had a distinctly human direction; it was a quest by a hungry band of frontiersmen who represent all that Steinbeck loved best in the American past. The impetus behind the westering movement "had its roots not in the flesh but in the human spirit," and it is, in fact, the passing of that spirit of movement from an America in which every frontier has been conquered that Steinbeck laments in "The Leader of the People."

What emerges in "The Leader of the People" is Steinbeck's identification and evaluation of a uniquely human group in which individual purposive goals are realized through collective action. This same belief in the value which can accrue to the individual from group involvement functions on a much larger scale in *The Grapes of Wrath*, in which the Joads, under Casy's guidance, realize that joint participation in a group movement (phalanx) aimed toward an agrarian ideal is necessary not only to ensure biological survival, but also to the moral end of affirming individual dignity.

The Theme of Life and Death

Arnold L. Goldsmith

Arnold L. Goldsmith analyzes the connecting themes and structural elements that integrate the four stories in *The Red Pony.* The stories, which cover two years in Jody Tiflin's life, take place on the Tiflin ranch in Salinas Valley, California. According to Goldsmith, Jody matures as he is forced to accept the realities of death and life of horses and of men. Arnold L. Goldsmith, who taught English at Wayne State University in Detroit, Michigan, is the author of scholarly articles on Oliver Holmes, Herman Melville, Henry James, and Frank Norris and is co-editor of the 1958 *Publication Guide for Literary and Linguistic Scholars.*

Underlying Steinbeck's four short stories which make up *The Red Pony* are thematic rhythms, structural balance, and a seasonal symbolism which skillfully integrate the whole work and relate it to his Emersonian mysticism found in later books such as *The Grapes of Wrath* (1939) and *Sea of Cortez* (1941). "The Leader of the People," added by Steinbeck in 1938 to the three stories first published as *The Red Pony* in 1937, is an integral part of the whole work, but readers of college anthologies usually find one of the stories published separately or the first three as a unit, and thus miss a good opportunity to study Steinbeck's subtle extension of the themes expressed in "The Gift," "The Great Mountains," and "The Promise."

The central figure unifying all four stories is Jody Tiflin. Like [American writer Ernest] Hemingway's early hero Nick Adams, Jody is being initiated into a violent world where danger lurks everywhere, pain and death are imminent, and the best laid plans of mice and boys often go astray. In the

Reprinted from Arnold L. Goldsmith, "Thematic Rhythm in *The Red Pony," College English*, February 1965, vol. 26. Copyright © 1965 by the National Council of Teachers of English. Reprinted with permission.

first story Jody is ten, in the next apparently a year older, and in the third and fourth, probably twelve. The adventures of both youths are intended to teach them the need for stoic endurance in order to survive in an imperfect and cruel world. In this sense, Hemingway's stories and *The Red Pony* can be considered *bildungsromans*,[1] but there are some significant differences. Because of Jody's age, sex plays much less a part of his initiation than it does in Nick's, whose experiences are not just vicarious. And violence, which explodes all around Nick and finally wounds him in the war, destroys only the things Jody loves, not harming him physically. Where Nick's wound are both physical and psychic, Jody's are only psychic, and we do not know whether they have a permanent effect on him. The third story ends with Jody's thrill at the birth of his new colt, but even this thrill is dampened by pain: "He ached from his throat to his stomach. His legs were stiff and heavy. He tried to be glad because of the colt, but the bloody face, and the haunted, tired eyes of Billy Buck hung in the air ahead of him." The last story substitutes the tired face of Jody's grandfather for that of Billy Buck, but the optimism implied in the title as well as Jody's kindness to the old man are adequate evidence of the kind of adjustments Jody will make in life.

UNITY OF PLACE AND TIME

More important than the above contrasts is the fact that Steinbeck composed *The Red Pony* as an integrated whole, while Hemingway wrote the Nick Adams stories sporadically at different times during his literary career. All four stories in *The Red Pony* take place in the Salinas Valley, where Steinbeck himself grew up as a boy. The stories are filled with realistic and lyric descriptions of the Valley's flora and fauna (*e.g.,* horned toads, newts, blue snakes, lizards, buzzards, rabbits, hoot-owls, turkeys, coyotes, muskmelons, oakwoods, and black cypresses) which Steinbeck knew as intimately as [American writer Henry David] Thoreau knew the woods, ponds, and fields around Concord [, Massachusetts].

The time sequence of the stories can be worked out as follows. "The Gift" begins in late summer and ends around Thanksgiving, the beginning of the winter with its rainy season in California. The reader of Hemingway's *A Farewell to Arms* is certainly familiar with the association of rain with

---

1. stories about the development of young characters

disease, violence, and death, and such seasonal symbolism is most appropriate in the story about the death of Jody's pony suffering from pneumonia. "The Great Mountains" begins in the "heat of a mid-summer afternoon," probably a year after the first story began. It spans less than twenty-four hours, ending the next morning. "The Promise" begins that spring and ends eleven months later, in a January rain, once again an appropriate setting for the death of the mare Nellie and the birth of her colt. "The Leader of the People" takes place a couple of months later, in March, probably the same year that the mare died. The same unity of time and place found in the second story is evident here also. As in "The Great Mountains," the story begins on an afternoon and ends the next morning.

This analysis of the time sequence helps illuminate the structural symmetry of the stories. Just as Hemingway in *A Farewell to Arms* alternates a book of war with a romantic interlude for dramatic contrast, Steinbeck follows the violence of the first story with the tragic quiet of the second, with this same pattern repeated in the third and fourth sections. Where the first and third stories are about the violent deaths of horses, the second and fourth are about the twilight years of two old men.

RHYTHMS AND CYCLES

The basic thematic rhythm unifying the four stories in *The Red Pony* is the life-death cycle. This organic theory of life ending in death which in turn produces new life is the major theme of Hemingway's "Indian Camp," where Nick Adams witnesses the Caesarean delivery of an Indian baby and the violent death of the father. It is the same cycle of life and death implicit in [American poet Walt] Whitman's image of the "cradle endlessly rocking."

In *The Red Pony* we see this rhythm in the cycle of the seasons, the buzzards flying overhead, the life and death of Jody's pony Gabilan, the death of the buzzard Jody kills with his bare hands, the approaching death of the paisano[2] Gitano and the old horse Easter (his very name suggesting life in death), and the two opposing sets of mountains: Gabilan (jolly, populated, suggesting life) and the Great Ones (ominous, mysterious, suggesting death, a place where we must all go eventu-

2. peasant

ally), the little bird Jody kills with his slingshot and then beheads and dissects, the death of Nellie and the birth of her colt, and the approaching death of Jody's old grandfather, the old leader of the people, with the implication that Jody is to be the new one. All of these objects and incidents represent the never-ending rhythm of life and death to which Jody is continually exposed. The subtle expression of this theme can even be found at the beginning of "The Leader of the People," when Billy Buck rakes the last of the old year's haystack, an action which implies the end of one season and the beginning of the next. In terms of the story, life is ending for the grandfather, but it is just beginning for Jody.

The most obvious example of Steinbeck's conscious effort to present this theme in *The Red Pony* is the sharp contrast he develops in "The Promise" between the black cypress tree by the bunkhouse and the water tub. Where the cypress is associated with death, the never-ending spring water piped into the old green tub is the symbol of the continuity of life. The two paragraphs where Steinbeck explains the effect these things have on Jody should be given in full:

> Jody traveled often to the brush line behind the house. A rusty iron pipe ran a thin stream of water into an old green tub. Where the water spilled over and sank into the ground there was a patch of perpetually green grass. Even when the hills were brown and baked in the summer that little patch was green. The water whined softly into the trough all the year round. This place had grown to be a center-point for Jody. When he had been punished the cool green grass and the singing water soothed him. When he had been mean the biting acid of meanness left him at the brush line. When he sat in the grass and listened to the purling stream, the barriers set up in his mind by the stern day went down to ruin.

> On the other hand, the black cypress tree by the bunkhouse was as repulsive as the water-tub was dear; for to this tree all the pigs came, sooner or later, to be slaughtered. Pig killing was fascinating, with the screaming and the blood, but it made Jody's heart beat so fast that it hurt him. After the pigs were scalded in the big iron tripod kettle and their skins were scraped and white, Jody had to go to the water-tub to sit in the grass until his heart grew quiet. The water-tub and the black cypress were opposites and enemies.

As Jody daydreams about his colt, he finds himself under the black cypress and superstitiously moves over to the green grass near the trilling water. "As usual the water place eliminated time and distance."

MYSTICAL CONNECTIONS TO NATURE

Jody's communion with nature, a semi-mystical experience in which time and place are eliminated, is not very different from the withdrawal into the wilderness of Jim Casy in *The Grapes of Wrath*. Casy adds a religious dimension to the experience when he says, "There was the hills, an' there was me, an' we wasn't separate no more. We was one thing. An' that one thing was holy." The most explicit statement Steinbeck has made on this mystical feeling of oneness of the animate and inanimate is in *Sea of Cortez*, where he wrote:

> groups melt into ecological groups until the time when what we know as life meets and enters what we think of as non-life: barnacle and rock, rock and earth, earth and tree, tree and rain and air. And the units nestle into the whole and are inseparable from it. . . . And it is a strange thing that most of the feeling we call religious, most of the mystical outcrying which is one of the most prized and used and desired reactions of our species, is really the understanding and the attempt to say that man is related to the whole thing, related inextricably to all reality, known and unknowable. This is a simple thing to say, but the profound feeling of it made a Jesus, a St. Augustine, a St. Francis, a Roger Bacon, a Charles Darwin, and an Einstein. Each of them in his own tempo and with his own voice discovered and reaffirmed with astonishment the knowledge that all things are one thing and that one thing is all things.

Throughout his literary career John Steinbeck has attempted to render dramatically his passionate belief in the oneness of all life, and *The Red Pony* is no exception, as the life-death cycle and Jody's romantic communion with nature will attest. But there is one final example which should be mentioned because of its effective fusion of character, theme, and setting. It occurs in "The Great Mountains." To Jody, these mountains represent the mystery of the unknown, unlived life, but to the old man they stand for the mystery of death. Beyond them lies the sea—eternity. As Gitano rides off into the mountains, he carries a long rapier with a golden basket hilt, a family heirloom passed down to him by his father. This rapier adds just the right touch of myth and folklore to the ancient legend of an old man returning to his birthplace to die. It echoes the classic tradition of such weapons as the magical sword of King Arthur and Beowulf,[3] the shield of Achilles,[4] even the long rifle of Natty Bumppo.[5] To Jody, Gitano

---

3. warrior in the Anglo-Saxon epic *Beowulf* 4. warrior in the Greek epic *Iliad* 5. hero in James Fenimore Cooper's *Leatherstocking* series

is "mysterious like the mountains. There were ranges back as far as you could see, but behind the last range piled up against the sky there was a great unknown country. And Gitano was an old man, until you got to the dull dark eyes. And in behind them was some unknown thing." Thus the mountains are an extension of Gitano, and Gitano is an extension of the old horse with its ribs and hip-bones jutting out under its skin. All three objects blend into one as Jody watches them disappear in the distance, lying in the green grass near the water-tub, the symbol of timelessness:

> For a moment he thought he could see a black speck crawling up the farthest ridge. Jody thought of the rapier and Gitano. And he thought of the great mountains. A longing caressed him, and it was so sharp that he wanted to cry to get it out of his breast. He lay down in the green grass near the round tub at the brush line. He covered his eyes with his crossed arms and lay there a long time, and he was full of a nameless sorrow.

The Ambiguous Role of Nature

Richard E. Hart

Richard E. Hart argues that Steinbeck portrays a complex view of humans and their relationship to nature. On one hand, Jody's feelings in "The Great Mountains" seem to suggest that humans are part of nature. On the other hand, according to Hart, Steinbeck's humans assert their free will against the forces of nature, as illustrated by Grandfather in "The Leader of the People." Richard E. Hart, who teaches philosophy at Bloomfield College in Bloomfield, New Jersey, is the editor of *Ethics and the Environment* and coeditor of *Plato's Dialogues: The Dialogical Approach.*

I take strong exception to the fairly common charge, like that once made by [critic] Stanley Edgar Hyman in a review of the *Sea of Cortez* for the *New Republic,* that Steinbeck was simply preoccupied with "rambling philosophizing" for its own sake. His was simply too mature and serious an intellect to fall prey to idle musings or dilettantish posturing. [In an article for the *Steinbeck Review* critic] Gloria Gaither rightly says, "Any discussion of Steinbeck the social reformer, Steinbeck the artist/writer, Steinbeck the journeyer, Steinbeck the marine biologist, remains inconclusive without a deep appreciation for and genuine understanding of Steinbeck the philosopher."

An eloquent indication of Steinbeck's treatment of the relation between man and nature was captured, I believe, by Anders Österling, a permanent secretary of the Swedish Academy, in the presentation address (1962) that he delivered when Steinbeck was awarded the Nobel Prize: "But in him we find the American temperament also in his great feeling for nature, for the tilled soil, the wasteland, the

Excerpted from Richard E. Hart, "Steinbeck on Man and Nature: A Philosophical Reflection," in *Steinbeck and the Environment: Interdisciplinary Approaches* (Tuscaloosa: University of Alabama Press, 1997). Reprinted with permission.

mountains, and the ocean coasts, all an inexhaustible source of inspiration to Steinbeck in the midst of, and beyond, the world of human beings." The philosophically intriguing aspect of this observation, which will be elaborated here, is the phrase "in the midst of, and beyond." A great feeling for nature in the midst of the world of humans and beyond the world of humans—just what does this mean or imply?

STEINBECK GOES BEYOND SIMPLE NATURALISM

Steinbeck's early "California" fiction is typically described as firmly ensconced within the tradition of naturalism. His characters are seen as simple and "natural," and in terms of habits, idioms, customs, and experience, Steinbeck is obviously on intimate terms with them. Thus if they are both simple and "natural" (an alleged unity of labels that many philosophers, particularly metaphysicians, have readily embraced), so must he be. As Österling and countless others have noted, the early Steinbeck was a writer of the land and its natural inhabitants, morally disposed to the preservation of nature's integrity. He was, in his thinking and work, both a functional part of nature and a student/appreciator of nature. Yet he was no simple-minded sentimentalist (though he could be sentimental on other counts) or popularizing nature freak. His on-again, off-again university education and long collegial association with scientist and collector Ed Ricketts demonstrate that he was formally trained and experienced in the biological and marine sciences. But he superseded the inherent limits and understandings of science, complementing science with a deeply appreciative understanding of nature from aesthetic and philosophical perspectives. In other words, Steinbeck's naturalism was no simple, unidimensional matter. Nature for the scientist, the theologian, and the romantic may well be a rather clearly defined, unequivocal reality. But what becomes of nature, its conceptualization and presentation, in the hands of a passionate artist, trained scientist, spiritually inclined nonbeliever, occasional romantic and transcendentalist like Steinbeck? . . .

HUMANS AS PART OF AN INDIFFERENT NATURE

Inescapably, man is but one element among many interrelated elements within the system of nature—a discrete cog in the vast machine. Steinbeck articulated this fundamental insight when, in the *Log from the Sea of Cortez*, he summarized his cosmic worldview in these words: "All things are one thing and . . . one thing is all things—plankton, a shimmering phosphorescence on the sea, and the spinning planets and an expanding universe, all bound together by the elastic string of time. It is advisable to look from the tide pool to the stars and then back to the tide pool again."

One might be tempted to say that nature, poetically or spiritually rendered, is man's true source, an authentic home, a kindly, albeit amoral, friend and nurturer that treats persons neutrally rather than cruelly as other people all too often seem to do when they crave money or power over values. For instance, consider such ambivalent longings for nature as George and Lennie's dream in *Of Mice and Men* of lasting solace on their never-to-be-realized couple of acres ("An' live off the fatta the lan'") or boy Jody's desire in "The Red Pony" to be absorbed into the mysterious, comforting though scary mountains, those taller, darker Santa Lucias, "Curious secret mountains . . . when the sun had gone over the edge in the evening and the mountains were a purple-like despair, then Jody was afraid of them."

But yet another, complementary dimension of "philosophical naturalism" is also, it turns out, central to Steinbeck's ideas about man and nature. Moreover, when we consider the claims of scholars such as Edwin H. Cady and Warren French ("Naturalism seems to fit only theoretical examples of a misguided theory"), this aspect of philosophical naturalism serves as a much-needed corrective to the narrow and impossible confines of literary naturalism (cited in Bloom 1987[1]). While it may well be that, from the scientist's perspective, the natural universe as a whole operates according to neutral, indifferent forces of cause and effect, nature nonetheless contains within it unique value-bearing, value-creating, value-acting sorts of entities, namely, human beings.

HUMANS CAN ALSO ACT DELIBERATELY

Humans both have and constantly pursue values through deliberation and action. Though a distinctive biological unit within the natural order, man is never wholly reducible in any way to the other parts or categories of nature. Signifi-

1. Harold Bloom is editor of *Modern Critical Views: John Steinbeck*.

cantly, man is *both* the same and different. To the extent that human persons, unique in status and function, engage in acts of valuing they reflect at least a measure of free will, they become "moral" beings, and thus must accept responsibility for choices and actions. Among all the elements constitutive of nature, only man can and does rise up against determinism through an exercise of will and moral consciousness. . . .

For Steinbeck, to be a human person is tantamount to being caught in a paradox, to be engaged, sometimes unwittingly, in living with and working through the dilemma of being at once both a determined unit of nature and a free, value-articulating individual forever called upon to act. In a vivid, existential sense, Steinbeck's fiction thus articulates through art the "lived experience" of the complexities and paradoxes of naturalism.

So man is in fact both free and not free, an apparently unassailable truth about the human condition, a reality philosophers have labeled "soft determinism" as a counterbalance to inflexible "hard determinism." In Steinbeck the blend is between his "scientific mechanism" and "humanistic vitalism" and follows logically from his empirically derived theory of "nonteleological thinking," which concerns itself with what "is" the case rather than what "could," "should," or "might" be. As a determined product of environment, in the broadest sense, individuals sometimes cannot help themselves, cannot be or do otherwise.

STEINBECK PORTRAYS BOTH THE DETERMINISM OF NATURE *AND* HUMAN FREE WILL

It thus comes as no surprise that Steinbeck's characters are often cast as though they are in an epical struggle with fickle nature or even their own uncontrollable passions and instincts. While a truthful claim about man and his condition, this *alone* could not suffice for Steinbeck, for it would imply that the characters, and their creator, the naturalistic writer, cannot attempt any moral judgments and must necessarily be inclined toward pessimism. Contrarily, in Steinbeck's work we witness the intersection, the complementarity, of the determinism of nature *and* man's freedom of existence, in other words, both scientific "cause and effect" and nonteleological "is" thinking. Simplistic or reductionistic models of naturalism will not do, for they either bury man in nature or seek to separate him from it. Philosophically and aesthetically, Steinbeck can be both an environmental determinist, broadly construed, and a "humanist" whose characters illustrate strong ethical qualities of choice and action.

Over and against the at times overwhelming forces of nature and fate, many of Steinbeck's early characters embody a compensating humanistic value that affirms the significance of the individual person no matter how lowly or seemingly ill equipped for the world. Man thus reveals a subtle kind of moral grandeur in his everyday life, in relations among common people such as gamblers, ranch hands, drunks, prostitutes, migrant laborers. Difficult though it may be, man *can* help himself through an act of will, thereby affirming the primacy of human dignity. In this respect, one cannot ignore Steinbeck's affinity with the idealism of American transcendentalists[2] such as [Ralph Waldo] Emerson, [Henry David] Thoreau, and [Walt] Whitman who tend to portray man as simultaneously individualistic and selflessly altruistic.

If the preceding is at all an accurate account, it is easy to see how for Steinbeck nature could be ambiguously conceived as both friend and enemy and, in turn, man himself variously celebrated for his courage and moral conquests (e.g., *In Dubious Battle*) and berated for his crass self-interest and sought-after superiority over nature (consider, e.g., the commercialization and abuse of the land and its people in *The Grapes of Wrath*). Man at times displays his *freedom* through moral grandeur and, at other times, through wanton hubris[3] against the forces of nature that frustrate his ambitions. For a telling illustration, simply recall (in "The Red Pony") boy Jody's grandfather describing that "line of old men along the shore hating the ocean because it stopped them" from their onward push to the west, from the "westering" that was their very modus operandi.[4]...

In sum, the philosophical naturalism embodied in Steinbeck's early and best fiction reflects an understanding of and faith in both nature and man. It is a complex and sophisticated outlook that can, in Socratic fashion, assist in greater self-understanding (the Delphic oracle's most enduring command was "know thyself").

2. Transcendentalism was a philosophy popular in New England in the 1800s, a philosophy relying on intuition and conscience. 3. excessive pride 4. usual way of operating

CHAPTER 2

Characters in *The Red Pony*

READINGS ON
THE RED PONY

The Education of a Young Boy

Peter Lisca

According to Peter Lisca, Jody Tiflin's education gives continuity to the four stories in *The Red Pony*. In the first three Jody learns about the nature of death, at times violent and painful, at times calm and peaceful, and at other times the price paid for life. From his grandfather's story, Jody learns the value of history, that meaning comes from the past. Peter Lisca, who taught English at the University of Florida, is the author of *John Steinbeck: Nature and Myth*, editor of a critical edition of *The Grapes of Wrath*, and author of many articles on modern American fiction.

Although the four stories about Jody do not have plot continuity, they do have a continuity of theme—the education of a young boy. The three stories collected in the 1937 edition of *The Red Pony* show Jody's education through Nature, and "The Leader of the People" continues this education through Grandfather, who represents history, a sense of the past. Like [Steinbeck's short story] "Flight," these stories are remarkable for the lyric realism of their prose style, a style which while coming to grips with the essentials of violence and death still retains a rhythm and tone more akin to the idyllic and pastoral than to the naturalistic. The result of this rhythm and tone is the creation of what [critic] T.K. Whipple has called "the middle distance." In this perspective the characters "cannot touch us, and yet we can see their performances with the greatest clarity and fullness. . . . We feel the appropriate emotions—pity, sympathy, terror and horror even—but with the delightful sense that we are apart, in the audience, and that anyhow nothing can be done or needs be done." This effect is very important in Steinbeck's work, and its presence is often a touchstone for his more successful

Excerpted from Peter Lisca, *The Wide World of John Steinbeck* (Brunswick, NJ: Rutgers University Press, 1958). Copyright © 1958 by Rutgers, The State University. Reprinted by permission of Rutgers University Press.

works. It is through this technique of distance that the stories about Jody escape both the infantilism and the excessive psychological distortions which are the usual literary pitfalls of these stories' subject matter.

"The Gift"

The central experience in each of the first three stories ("The Gift," "The Great Mountains," and "The Promise") is physical death: the red pony, Gitano, and the mare. Each shows death in a different perspective. The red pony comes from a broken-down "show," and its superficial prettiness is emphasized by the tinsel-hung, red morocco saddle that comes with it. "'It's just a show saddle,' Billy Buck said disparagingly. 'It isn't practical for the brush. . . .'" The red pony's death is in part the result of Jody's carelessness. Twice he falls asleep and allows the pony to escape into the storm, which aggravates the cold it caught from getting wet. Billy Buck has remarked, "—why a little rain don't hurt a horse." But it is fatal to the red pony. When Jody comes upon his red pony, already being devoured by the buzzards, anger seems a normal reaction. Carl Tiflin says, "Jody, the buzzards didn't kill the pony. Don't you know that?" The function of this incident in Jody's education becomes clear from Billy Buck's reprimand. "'Course he knows it, Jesus Christ! man, can't you see how he'd feel about it?" It is important to note that he does not contradict the father's words, but merely relates Jody's action to its context of incomplete education. The reader may "feel" with Jody and "understand" with Carl, but he identifies himself with Billy Buck, the complete man whose perspective includes both the buzzards' place in the chain of being and their repulsiveness. And Billy Buck is the model on whom Jody is fashioning himself.

"The Great Mountains"

While the death of the red pony is associated with violence, pain, and disgust, the death of Gitano in "The Great Mountains" is as calm and peaceful as the title. Before the old Mexican comes "home" to the Tiflin ranch to die, Jody has already identified the western mountains, the "Great Ones," with death and the eastern ones, the Gabilans, with life. Symbolically, the Tiflin ranch lies in a valley cup formed by the two ranges. When Gitano disappears with the old horse, Easter, who is also waiting to die, Carl remarks, "They never get too old to steal. I guess he just stole old Easter." Jody, who has seen

Gitano's old basket-hilted rapier (handed down from father to son since the conquistadores), who feels the significance of Gitano's journey into the symbolic "Great Ones," knows the truth. "Jody thought of the rapier and of Gitano. And he thought of the great mountains. A longing caressed him, and it was so sharp that he wanted to cry to get it out of his breast. He lay down in the green grass near the round tub [which Jody associates with life] at the brush line. He covered his eyes with his crossed arms and lay there a long time, and he was full of nameless sorrow." This sorrow comes not from grief for Gitano or the old horse, but rather from an emotional perception of that whole of which Gitano, Old Easter, the rapier, and the Great Mountains are parts, a recognition of the symbolic significance of their conjunction—"nameless" because intuitive and subconscious. Jody's sorrow is very much like that of the girl Margaret in [British poet Gerard Manley] Hopkins' poem "Spring and Fall: To a Young Child."

"THE PROMISE"

Like "The Gift," "The Promise" is a story about a pony. Whereas the first concerns itself with the pony's increasing sickness, ending in death, the second begins with a pony's conception and ends with its birth. And as Jody was spared no detail of the first pony's suffering and death, so he is spared no fact of life in the mare's pregnancy and the colt's birth. He is present at the violent copulation, cares for the mare during the progress of her pregnancy, sees the agonies of her labor pains, watches Billy Buck attempt to turn the colt in her uterus and, this failing, kill her with a hammer and cut the living colt from its dead mother. Jody's vital relation to this colt is as different from his relation to the red pony as the red pony's carnival background and useless red morocco saddle are different from the violence and suffering which bring the colt into the world. And the colt's birth provides Jody with a new insight into death. The red pony's suffering and terror had been the process of death, which meant life to the buzzards. Gitano had gone to his death calmly, of his own free will and accepting the inevitable. The mare's suffering and death are the price of life and give to Jody a new sense of his responsibility to that life.

In *Sea of Cortez* Steinbeck tells an anecdote, probably autobiographical, which further clarifies his attitude toward the natural processes of life in these Jody stories:

A man we know once long ago worked for a wealthy family in a country place. One morning one of the cows had a calf. The children of the house went down with him to watch her. It was a good normal birth, a perfect presentation, and the cow needed no help. The children asked questions and he answered them. And when the emerged head cleared through the sac, the little black muzzle appeared, and the first breath was drawn, the children were fascinated and awed. And this was the time for their mother to come screaming down on the vulgarity of letting the children see the birth. This "vulgarity" had given them a sense of wonder at the structure of life, while the mother's propriety supplanted that feeling with dirtiness.

Because the style of the Jody stories is so perfectly suited to their theme and subject matter (as well suited, for example, as is the style of *The Pearl* to its own materials), the myriad specific details imbedded in these stories remain unobtrusive. Jody, however, is engaged in learning not only about such larger things as death, birth, and suffering, but also about the many particulars of ranch life and nature. The source for much of this information is Billy Buck, who, along with other men of skill, occupies the place in the Steinbeck world that bullfighters do in that of [American writer Ernest] Hemingway. Throughout his fiction Steinbeck pays tribute to the man who is skilled with his hands: the man who can, like Billy Buck and Slim, work with horses; the man who can, like Raymond Banks, kill chickens painlessly and with efficiency; the man who can, like Alec and Juan Chicoy, repair motors and gear assemblies. In *Cannery Row* Steinbeck refers to Gay, a self-made mechanic, as "the Saint Francis of all things that turn and twist and explode." This type of character is often depicted by Steinbeck, who thus expresses his admiration for the man who is close to life, whether that life be spent on a ranch, in a garage, or behind a lunch counter. In Doc of *Cannery Row* Steinbeck creates his ideal character by combining the man of skill with the man of contemplation.

"THE LEADER OF THE PEOPLE"

While the boy Jody appears in "The Leader of the People," it is not *about* him in the sense that the stories in *The Red Pony* are about him. This is why Steinbeck did not include this story in the first edition of *The Red Pony*, although he had probably written it by then since it is found in the same manuscript book as the earlier *Tortilla Flat*, "The Murder," and "The Chrysanthemums," where it is called "Grandfather." Although this story was later included in the 1945 edition of *The Red Pony,* in *The Long Valley* (1938) it appears under a separate title. The central character is Jody's grandfather, who was once "the leader of the people." It is Steinbeck's first explicit statement of his group-man theory, which was hinted at in the earlier stories and novels and which was to be developed at such great length in his next four books.

Through the garrulous grandfather Steinbeck poses the question of the meaning and place which the frontier spirit should have in our time. Through each character's attitude toward the grandfather, in whom the tradition is embodied, the author explores a distinct reaction to the American pioneer past. For Carl, it is something done with. The West Coast has been reached and the job now is one of consolidation. It is boring and pointless to dwell on the heroic deeds of our past: "Now it's finished. Nobody wants to hear about it over and over." In this dismissal there is perhaps an unconscious resentment of his own unheroic life. To Carl's wife, the daughter of Grandfather, the stories of the past are just as boring, but her attitude is more respectful. She listens out of loyalty, knowing what this past meant to her forebears. Billy Buck's attitude is a little more complicated. His own father was a mule packer under Grandfather's leadership, and he himself retains much of the self-reliant, ablehanded spirit of the heroic past. He listens with respect born of understanding. For Jody, as for any other American youngster, this past was a time of excitement: Indians, wagon trains, scouts, crossing the plains.

Yet it is to Jody that the grandfather is finally able to communicate the double aspect of the meaning behind his tales of Indians and wagon trains: "It wasn't Indians that were important, nor adventures, nor even getting out here. It was a whole bunch of people made into one big crawling beast. And I was the head. It was westering and westering. Every man wanted something for himself, but the big beast that was all of them wanted only westering. I was the leader, but if I hadn't been there, someone else would have been the head. The thing had to have a head." This is an important statement for an understanding of Steinbeck's group-man concept. The analogy of men to a "big crawling beast" was not intended to put, and in the context of Steinbeck's work does not put, men on the same moral basis as animals.

Rather, it points out the energy that is released when the many desires of men can find expression in one unifying activity or aspiration. As the old man continues, it becomes evident that although "westering" may bear a superficial resemblance to animal migration, the impetus which drove his people had its roots not in the flesh but in the human spirit. "No place to go, Jody. Every place is taken. But that's not the worst—no, not the worst. Westering has died out of people. Westering isn't a hunger any more. It's all done."

Grandfather's statement is supported not only by Carl Tiflin and his wife, but by a continuum of symbols firmly imbedded in the story. The physical setting is alive not with Indians and buffaloes but with small and petty game—gophers, snakes, pigeons, crows, rabbits, squirrels, and mice. And these mice which Jody sets out to kill early in the story are, significantly, still alive at its end, fat and comfortable in a rotting haystack. Yet, the story is not a sentimental glorification of a heroic past set against a mean and complacent present. The frontier *is* gone; Jody's excitement about killing the mice is not, as Grandfather sees it, a symbol of a degenerating race; Carl Tiflin and his wife are not cruel and stupid, but competent for the tasks at hand; and their boredom with the old man's garrulousness is made understandable. Furthermore, in a very important sense it is Grandfather who has failed, in two ways. He has failed to adjust himself to the unavoidable fact that he could not go on being "the leader of the people" after the Pacific Ocean was reached. More important, despite his garrulousness he has failed to communicate to the new generation that "westering" was not just killing Indians and eating buffalo meat.

Perhaps the ultimate wisdom in the story belongs only to Billy Buck. When Jody remarks to him that the fat mice he intends to kill "don't know what's going to happen to them today," Billy Buck replies philosophically, "No, nor you either, nor me, nor anyone." Jody is "staggered" by this thought; he "knew it was true." This is Jody's lesson in history, the meaning of the past. Grandfather's frontier, like [historian] Frederick Jackson Turner's, was not so much a physical manifestation as an attitude of mind and a spirit which needs reviving in our time. Life is always a risk. The call for heroism is heard today as it was yesterday. The need for a leader of the people is still real, for we are all pioneers, forever crossing the dangerous and the unknown.

Jody's Initiation into Adulthood

F.W. Watt

According to F.W. Watt, *The Red Pony* is about Jody's initiation into the world of adulthood: "The four episodes lead the boy Jody through stages of initiation into the mysteries which the adult must live with: sickness, age, death, procreation, and birth." F.W. Watt's research includes studies of the early and late works of John Steinbeck and an overview of Steinbeck criticism.

"The Red Pony" is a loosely-connected sequence of four stories: their link is the boy Jody who is a central figure in each, and who has obvious autobiographical associations. There is an air of intimate, personal revelation about this sequence which we rarely find elsewhere in Steinbeck, and which partly accounts for its freshness and immediacy. Looking back in 1953, Steinbeck said: "*The Red Pony* was written a long time ago, when there was desolation in my family. The first death had occurred. And the family, which every child believes to be immortal, was shattered. Perhaps this is the first adulthood of any man or woman. The first tortured question 'Why?' and then acceptance, and then the child becomes a man. *The Red Pony* was an attempt, an experiment if you wish, to set down this loss and acceptance and growth." This is a revealing comment; but the power of the sequence lies in the fact that it portrays the "loss and acceptance and growth" in a concrete way without abstract discussion or moral conclusion. The potent symbolism is perfectly natural, and the characters have the rounded presences of real life: Jody, "a little boy, ten years old, with hair like dusty yellow grass and with shy polite grey eyes and with a mouth that worked when he thought"; his father, Carl Tiflin, a stern disciplinarian who hates weakness, sick-

Excerpted from F.W. Watt, *Steinbeck* (Edinburgh: Oliver & Boyd, 1962).

ness, and helplessness; his mother, who expresses her tenderness only in practical domestic ways; and the cowhand Billy Buck, Jody's idol: "a broad, bandy-legged little man with a walrus moustache, with square hands, puffed and muscled on the palms. His eyes were a contemplative, watery grey and the hair which protruded from under his Stetson hat was spiky and weathered." Billy Buck is a gruff, blunt, practical man, wise in the ways of cattle, horses, and little boys. The relationship and interaction of these four is presented with subtlety and vividness.

The four episodes lead the boy Jody through stages of initiation into the mysteries which the adult must live with: sickness, age, death, procreation, birth. On the farm Jody learns to associate the two opposite forces of experience, life-bringing and death-bringing, with the water-spring and the cypress tree near the house. Spring-water ran in a thin stream out of a rusty iron pipe into an old green tub, spilling over and soaking into the ground. There the grass was permanently green, and the cold greenness and the sound of the water comforted the boy. By contrast the nearby black cypress tree was ominous and repulsive: under its branches all the pigs were brought in turn to be slaughtered, after which they were scalded in the big iron kettle, and their skins scraped white. Fascinated and horrified, Jody would have to return to the flowing spring-water to be soothed.

JODY'S INITIATION INTO THE FACT OF DEATH

"The Gift" tells of Jody's new red pony which takes sick and dies despite even Billy Buck's practical skill; the horror of Jody's struggle with the ugly buzzard, which he catches devouring the dead pony, projects his revulsion against the fact of death, and the different reactions of Carl and Billy are subtly conveyed. "His father moved the buzzard [which Jody has killed] with his toe. 'Jody,' he explained, 'the buzzard didn't kill the pony. Don't you know that?' 'I know it,' Jody said wearily. It was Billy Buck who was angry. He had lifted Jody in his arms, and had turned to carry him home. But he turned back on Carl Tiflin. "Course he knows it,' Billy said furiously, 'Jesus Christ! man, can't you see how he'd feel about it?'" In "The Great Mountains," again, natural symbolism plays a strong part, and again the quality of Billy's understanding is played off against Carl Tiflin's, as Jody's experience is deepened. To the east of the valley are the

THE MOUNTAINS AND THE VALLEY

The western mountains both entice and threaten Jody, the eastern Gabilans offer him joy and human activity, and the valley represents a safe and warm world.

That was all the information Jody ever got, and it made the mountains dear to him, and terrible. He thought often of the miles of ridge after ridge until at last there was the sea. When the peaks were pink in the morning they invited him among them: and when the sun had gone over the edge in the evening and the mountains were a purple-like despair, then Jody was afraid of them; then they were so impersonal and aloof that their very imperturbability was a threat.

Now he turned his head toward the mountains of the east, the Gabilans, and they were jolly mountains, with hill ranches in their creases, and with pine trees growing on the crests. People lived there, and battles had been fought against the Mexicans on the slopes. He looked back for an instant at the Great Ones and shivered a little at the contrast. The foothill cup of the home ranch below him was sunny and safe. The house gleamed with white light and the barn was brown and warm. The red cows on the farther hill ate their way slowly toward the north. Even the dark cypress tree by the bunkhouse was usual and safe. The chickens scratched about in the dust of the farmyard with quick waltzing steps.

John Steinbeck, *The Red Pony*. New York: Viking, 1945.

"jolly" Gabilan mountains with their populated creases and foothills; to the west the Great Mountains, dark, savage, empty of life, mysterious and terrible to the mind. The old paisano[1] man who comes to the Tiflin ranch, his birthplace years before Tiflin's time, to end his days there, responds to Tiflin's callous rebuff by walking off to die in the Great Mountains, "stealing" Carl's equally old and useless horse to take with him. Carl is merely amused and bewildered, but Jody, with an overwhelming sadness, senses the old man's feeling and purpose. "The Promise" follows on from "The Gift." Having lost the red pony, Jody is promised a new colt, which this time is not merely a gift, a pretty circus horse: he has responsibility from the moment of conception—watching the stallion savagely mounting the mare Nellie and then caring for the mare until the birth. But the birth so much wished-for is a terrible experience; Billy Buck has to destroy

1. peasant

the mare to save the colt: "Billy's face and arms and chest were dripping red. His body shivered and his teeth chattered. His voice was gone; he spoke in a throaty whisper: 'There's your colt, I promised. And there it is. I had to do it—had to.'" Birth and death are inextricably related for Jody. "He tried to be glad because of the colt, but the bloody face, and the haunted, tired eyes of Billy Buck hung in the air ahead of him."

THE HOPE OF HEROISM

"The Leader of the People" is in an altogether different mood. Jody is once again initiated into a mystery—that of history. Jody's grandfather lives in the memory of the challenge and adventure of his own exciting past as a western pioneer, and bores his son-in-law Carl Tiflin with repeated tales of the heroic wagon-trail trek of a generation earlier. Jody is fascinated by the tales of heroic feats and battles with the Indians, but to Carl this age is simply over and finished: it means nothing to him. Jody is present when the old man at last realises he has been making a fool of himself; it is a significant awakening: "Westering has died out of the people. Westering isn't a hunger any more. It's all done." The fact that only the little boy is there to listen confirms this conclusion; but the eagerness in Jody's eyes denies it. The heroic days are over, but not the craving for heroism.

The Role of Billy Buck

Robert M. Benton

While recounting the major events in the four stories, Robert M. Benton stresses Steinbeck's use of nature. Both the detailed description of the ranch atmosphere and the natural events of birth and death
teach Jody about life. Jody's most direct education,
however, comes from the "natural man," Billy Buck,
who understands Jody as his father does not. Robert
M. Benton's research includes studies of Steinbeck's
early works and the works of other writers of American naturalism.

Critics have universally praised *The Red Pony* as containing
Steinbeck's best writing. Its appeal to both the young and the
old rests upon its general theme of the maturing of a young
boy, handled with a deftness seldom achieved in the twentieth
century. The story of *The Red Pony* is given in four parts,
published at various intervals between 1933 and 1938. Although each section can stand alone, it is fitting to consider
them consecutively. It is the story of Jody Tiflin, and it is also
the story of John Steinbeck whose statement concerning the
story [in *My Short Novels*] sets its context:

> *The Red Pony* was written a long time ago, when there was
> desolation in my family. The first death occurred. And the
> family, which every child believes to be immortal, was shat-
> tered. Perhaps this is the first adulthood of any man or
> woman. The first tortured question 'Why?' and then accep-
> tance, and then the child becomes a man. *The Red Pony* was
> an attempt, an experiment if you wish, to set down this loss
> and acceptance and growth.

The first story in *The Red Pony*, "The Gift," is the best
known. Ten-year-old Jody lives on a farm in the Salinas Valley with his mother, his father Carl who is a strong disciplinarian, and Billy Buck the hired hand. One morning his
father shows him a red circus pony that is to be his, if he
takes care of him. Jody names the pony Gabilan, for the

Excerpted from Robert M. Benton, "Steinbeck's *The Long Valley*," in *A Study Guide to
John Steinbeck*, edited by Tetsumaro Hayashi (Methuchen, NJ: Scarecrow Press, 1974).
Reprinted with permission.

ever-present Gabilan Mountains, and Billy Buck helps Jody train him. Through carelessness, the pony is left in the rain, gets sick, and dies despite Billy Buck's tireless efforts to save Gabilan. Jody stays with the pony almost constantly, but he falls asleep and Gabilan leaves the barn. By the time Jody reaches the pony it is too late—the buzzards had already begun their work. In a frenzy of frustration Jody seizes a buzzard and beats it to death with a rock.

"The Gift" is moving solely through the physical action of the plot. Few readers can fail to respond to Jody's suffering, loss, and final acceptance. In addition, Steinbeck's description, especially that of "the grey quiet mornings when the land and the brush and the houses and the trees were silvergrey and black like a photograph negative," allows the reader to experience morning before the sun has roused the farm and its inhabitants. Throughout the story, Steinbeck's use of concrete images and his avoidance of abstractions create powerfully descriptive passages.

Although "The Gift" is focused primarily on Jody's education through nature, and death in nature, a secondary concern is equally evident. Carefully woven into the fabric of "The Gift" is a quite explicit comparison and contrast between Jody's father and Billy Buck. Jody's father makes the rules and demands obedience. "His father was a disciplinarian. Jody obeyed him in everything without questions of any kind." Even Carl's presents "were given with reservations which hampered their value somewhat. It was good discipline." But Jody does not learn from Carl; he learns from nature, and the natural man, Billy, guides him. Nowhere is this contrast more evident than the end of the story when Billy and Carl find Jody. Billy pulls Jody away from the dead buzzard and holds him to calm him. Carl can only say, "the buzzard didn't kill the pony. Don't you know that?" No one but natural man can sense the magnitude of Jody's grief and make an appropriate response.

"THE GREAT MOUNTAINS"

The second story, "The Great Mountains," provides a counterpoint to "The Gift." It is not the death of a pony but a human with which Jody is confronted. The boy first becomes aware of the mountains which enclose the farm. To the west are the big mountains, described by Carl as "dangerous, with cliffs and things." But to the east are the jolly

Gabilans. "People lived there, and battles had been fought against the Mexicans on the slopes. He looked back for an instant at the Great Ones and shivered a little at the contrast." Jody's thoughts are quickly changed by the approach of an old man who proclaims, "I am Gitano, and I have come back." He explained that he was born on that land, and he obviously had come home to die.

Carl's hard nature again is dramatized when he tells Gitano he will have to leave. "Go to your friends. Don't come to die with strangers." Jody is fascinated by the old man and responds with human compassion. He asks Gitano questions about the past and shows him the stock, including the thirty-year-old horse, Easter, that Carl says should be shot. "Old things ought to be put out of their misery. . . . One shot, a big noise, one big pain in the head maybe, and that's all. That's better than stiffness and sore teeth." The next morning Gitano is gone, having taken old Easter with him into the Great Mountains to die. The story is calm and almost peaceful, with none of the scenes of violence which appear in "The Gift." But Jody learns once more that death comes to all. Regardless of their past usefulness, old men and horses are discarded, and the realization fills Jody with "a nameless sorrow."

"The Promise"

The third story, "The Promise," plays upon the same motif as "The Gift." Having lost the red pony, Jody is promised Nellie's foal if he will work all summer to pay the five dollar stud fee. Jody is now involved from the moment of conception when he leads Nellie up the road where he fearfully watches Jess Taylor's stallion savagely mount the mare. He faithfully cares for Nellie, but the birth which he anticipated so long is a terrible experience. When the mare's time has come and she seems not able to give birth, Jody remembers that Billy Buck had failed with the pony too. Suddenly, Nellie is ready, but the foal is turned the wrong way. Jody refuses to leave the barn, but he does turn his head as Billy rips open the mare's belly and drags out the colt.

> Billy's face and arms and chest were dripping red. His body shivered and his teeth chattered. His voice was gone; he spoke in a throaty whisper. 'There's your colt. I promised. And there it is. I had to do it—had to.'

Again Jody has insight into nature and death. The mare dies to give new life. There is no fault to be reckoned in what has happened. In nature life and death are intimately bound together, and Jody's responsibility for the new colt is accompanied by his awareness of the interrelatedness of nature.

"THE LEADER OF THE PEOPLE"

"The Leader of the People," the fourth story of *The Red Pony*, has a different mood and for some a change in focus, but it fits compactly with the previous three. Jody Tiflin's grandfather, his *mother's* father, appears to be the central character in "The Leader of the People." The talkative old man retells his stories of leading wagon loads of families across hostile lands to the ocean, much to the consternation of Carl. As the tales continue, Carl becomes more irritable until he tells his wife, "Well, how many times do I have to listen to the story of the iron plates, and the thirty-five horses? That time's done. . . . Nobody wants to hear about it over and over." But the old man has overheard.

Carl feebly apologizes, but it does not cure Grandfather's pain. Grandfather admits that the tales are not what he wants to tell. "It wasn't Indians that were important, nor adventures, nor even getting out here. It was a whole bunch of people made into one big crawling beast. And I was the head." He wants those who hear his stories to feel, and only Jody can. It is Jody who knows the old man's deepest needs and who gives Grandfather reason to hope that at least one person felt as he wanted him to. In this sense, then, Jody may still be the central character in the story. [Critic Alfred H. Grommon says,] "Jody has already become a leader in showing his people a direction toward better understanding by first accepting the facts that exist. He, too, like his grandfather, fits Steinbeck's theory of leadership."

The four stories of *The Red Pony* are a fitting conclusion to *The Long Valley,* for they manifest some of the best writing of Steinbeck as well as some of the best American writing produced. When Steinbeck was awarded the Nobel Prize, the Committee said that it was awarded "For his at one and the same time realistic and imaginative writings, distinguished as they are by a sympathetic humor and social perception." No volume exemplifies the statement of the Nobel Committee as does *The Long Valley.* The stories in the volume will continue to stimulate readers' imaginations and will evoke thoughts and emotions which will contribute to the celebration of living.

CHAPTER 3

The Red Pony: Narrative Structure and Style

READINGS ON
THE RED PONY

Narrative Technique in *The Red Pony*

Howard Levant

Howard Levant analyzes Steinbeck's narrative technique, emphasizing that Steinbeck consistently tells the stories from Jody's point of view. Jody's telling conveys his own growing awareness that humans are imperfect and that tragedy and death are inevitable parts of life. Howard Levant taught English at Hartwick College in Oneonta, New York, before he became a full-time poet. He is the author of *The Novels of John Steinbeck: A Critical Study* and numerous articles on modern poetry and American culture.

The Red Pony is a very early and a completely successful instance of the organic relationship between structure and materials which distinguishes Steinbeck's most important fiction. It is set off from much of Steinbeck's work by a relative absence of extraneous devices intended to force order into the work of art.

NARRATIVE ELEMENTS FOCUS THE THEME OF JODY'S MATURATION

This long short story consists of three episodes: "The Gift," "The Great Mountains," and "The Promise." The structure is panoramic with a strong thematic unity which binds the three episodes together. Their shared reference is to one important experience, the process of growing up, and their shared focus is on one character, the boy Jody. The episodes provide concrete evidence that the meaning of growing up is chiefly a development of a sense that life and death are involved in each other; this awareness is equated with a growth of a sense of tragedy. Detail is presented consistently in terms of Jody's progressive awareness of the reality of death. The objective events and their implied meanings are self-contained.

Because Jody's is the point of view, we tend to accept his innocence as our own. The events are developed so that

Excerpted from Howard Levant, "John Steinbeck's *The Red Pony:* A Study in Narrative Technique," *The Journal of Narrative Technique*, vol. 1, no. 2 (Spring 1971). Reprinted with permission.

each episode is an objective record of Jody's experience and deepening awareness. One episode flows into the next, and the last episode fuses with the first because it ends as the first begins, with the present of a pony for Jody; but any sense of a purely mechanical progression is subordinated to Jody's innocent point of view.

There are some minor mechanical connections between characters and events which serve only to tighten the story. Thus, each episode begins with a focus on Jody's childish faith in adults or a child's game or daydream, but an adult problem intrudes and absorbs the child's world. The specific content in the process is that death and imperfection are everywhere, and that people try to conquer death and overcome imperfection in spite of their failures, while nature is a merely neutral element.

Death is a natural and fairly innocent presence in the opening division of "The Gift." Jody's world is ordered by kindly and severe adults, but contains cows and pigs that are to be butchered, a dog that has killed a coyote and been lamed, unseen dead animals, and highly visible buzzards. At night Jody hears owls hunting mice. Of all the evidence of death, Jody hates only the buzzards "as all decent things hate them." They are natural enough, and so necessary "they could not be hurt." Yet, in feeding on carrion, buzzards mark the point at which death becomes an ugly imperfection that cannot be accepted serenely. Buzzards prove that nature feeds on nature. They dramatize the ugly fact. And, within Jody's experience, their realistic function connotes their symbolic role at the conclusion—as the ultimate images of Death.

IMPERFECTION AND HAPPINESS INTERMIXED

Into this flawed ranch world, and into Jody's formless innocence, Jody's father brings the red pony. In keeping with the theme, the pony is not quite perfect. He is untrained, acquired at an auction after the bankruptcy of a "show." The red saddle he comes with is too frail for ordinary use, and he has been paid for by money from the butchered cows. Also this random gift emphasizes Mr. Tiflin's own imperfection. Jody's father is a stern disciplinarian, implicitly afraid to express his affection for Jody. Mr. Tiflin's materialistic gift and his claim that the pony will be useful mask his effort to express a love for Jody that he cannot express in words. The

ironies increase. Once he sees the red pony, Jody is filled
with wonder and affection for it, not for Mr. Tiflin, but the
pony bites Jody's hand.

These narrative details suggest a weight of imperfection,
but, for the moment, that weight is lifted by Jody's happiness. He loves the stylish red saddle and feels that biting
proves the pony's high spirits. Even the doubts of his play-
mates, when they learn the pony is untrained, fail to dimin-
ish Jody's happiness. He even rises somewhat out of childhood. When his friends leave, he speaks to the pony "in a
deep voice," and directs all of his attention to this new love;
and his mother points to this development when she feels "a
curious pride rise up in her" as she sees Jody falling in love
with the pony.

The pony's training can be read in abstract terms as the
bending of nature to man's will, or paralleled with Jody's
growing up, but the specific details of the training carry
their own conviction. The fact is that Billy Buck, the kindly
stable hand, teaches the pony with Jody's help; implicitly,
Billy teaches Jody how to be a man by way of using a horse
without showing fear. Still, the first time that Jody thinks of
riding the pony as a fact, he is afraid of being hurt if the pony
should fall. This reality merges with Jody's distanced fantasies of imperfection, for he imagines at times that the pony
has been hurt, but only to indulge the childish luxury of self-
torture. The final sentence in this passage sets aside fears
and fantasies; Jody's happiness is predominant: "When the
two came back from an expedition they smelled of the sweet
sage they had forced through." Nonetheless, happiness and
imperfection are so mingled in the details of this episode
that very often they cannot be separated. Jody's mother
speaks "irritably" and his father "crossly" to Jody on the
morning he gets the pony, since they do not know how to express the love or joy that they do feel. Jody's mother says to
Carl Tiflin, "Don't you let it keep him from school," and his
father "walked up a side-hill to be by himself, for he was embarrassed." Yet the objective narrator, not Jody, records
these details. Again, the pony connotes power, quite as
strongly as love, as when the visiting boys are awed: "They
knew instinctively that a man on a horse is spiritually as
well as physically bigger than a man on foot." And love is
balanced by the mixed stages of the training; the carrots and
the petting occur in a context of details such as this: "The

first time the pony wore the bridle he whipped his head about and worked his tongue against the bit until the blood oozed from the corners of his mouth . . . and his eyes turned red with fear and with general rambunctiousness. Jody rejoiced, for he knew that only a mean-souled horse does not resent training."

ILLNESS AND DEATH SUPERIMPOSED ON IMPERFECTION AND HAPPINESS

The illness and death of the pony occur in this context of imperfection that even happiness does not negate. The central human fact is that Jody tends to transfer an implicit belief in his father's perfection to the less awesome Billy Buck, who is aware that he cannot bear to seem fallible to Jody. Partly because of this self-knowledge, Billy claims too much good sense, and he is badly mistaken on three occasions. The pony gets wet because Billy misjudges the weather (by quiet irony it is near Thanksgiving, when Jody can ride the pony); the pony gets sick in spite of Billy's assurance that he will not; and the pony fails to get better in spite of Billy's careful doctoring. To complete the round, Jody's need to place the whole blame for human imperfection on Billy dissolves when Jody goes to sleep in the stable, while the pony might yet recover, and wakes up to find that the pony has wandered outdoors into the chilly night. Jody does not mention this lapse, but he falls asleep again and lets the pony wander off to its death.

Carl Tiflin, Billy Buck, and Jody Tiflin are imperfect, then, in their various human ways. But the ultimate fusion of death with imperfection (and a human striving after perfection) is presented in one brilliant narrative image in the final division of the episode, in Jody's fight with the buzzard. When Jody finds the pony's body, he catches one buzzard and beats it to death. Jody wishes to protect the dead pony because he was unable to protect the sick, living pony, but his "punishment" of the carrion eater is worse than futile. The imagery indicates that nature is an indifferent process to which men assign meaning. The buzzard cannot be hurt even by its death, for it is not human; as Jody struck, "the red fearless eyes still looked at him, impersonal and unafraid and detached." Carl Tiflin cannot understand Jody's act (or, probably, the foregoing image), so, in the last paragraph of the episode, Billy Buck expresses Jody's feelings: "His father moved the buzzard with his toe. 'Jody,' he explained, 'the buzzard didn't kill the pony. Don't you know that?' 'I know it,' Jody said wearily. It was Billy Buck who was angry. He had lifted Jody in his arms, and had turned to carry him home. But he turned back on Carl Tiflin. "Course he knows it,' Billy said furiously, 'Jesus Christ! man, can't you see how he'd feel about it?'" There is no loading of meaning; the passage's intensity and the shifts in tone are implicit in the objective narrative, as a sequence of human responses on the basis of everything that has gone before. Jody has learned that nothing can be blamed, given human imperfection and uncaring nature. The fallible but fatherly Billy Buck—Jody in his arms—being closer to nature, and more involved in Jody, can understand better than the well-meaning but detached Carl Tiflin, who presumes that Jody is inwardly as young as his physical age. The one positive touch is that Jody and Billy Buck share an awareness of human imperfection and of an impersonal nature.

STEINBECK'S DETAILS CONVEY JODY'S DEVELOPMENT

So, by a completely unspoken implication, Jody leaps into the sense of tragedy that defines manhood. As silently, that leap is an ironic by-product of the circumstances of the pony's illness and death. More than in much of his later work, Steinbeck is willing here to let an extensive texture of imagery, events, and characters produce their own implicit meanings. Steinbeck's later concept of "is" thinking (non-teleological observation[1]) is intended to produce a precise language; that precision is organically justified here because many of the details of the pony's training, illness, and death are new to Jody. And those details serve implicitly to indicate Jody's development from childish innocence to a mature, tragic awareness; they are not merely an aspect of Steinbeck's technique. Particularly Steinbeck avoids any suggestion of the allegory that is so common in the later novels. For example, the buzzards are really, and therefore organically, the chief images of Death that a country boy would know about. The imagistic richness of the Death figure is precisely its natural quality, which corresponds perfectly with its larger meaning. A buzzard is a natural and necessary beast, and a terrible one, and in these qualities it

1. a scientific, objective view

approximates our feelings about death itself. Hence the image grows out of its surroundings and fulfills its own nature; its objectivity precludes allegorical pumping.

MYSTERY, DEATH, AND THE SEARCH FOR A FATHER

The second episode, "The Great Mountains," is an interlude that continues a development of the themes of Death, imperfection, and a sense of tragedy, but with some decline of narrative intensity.

The episode begins with a seemingly aimless introduction. Jody plays around the ranch—he tortures the lamed dog that he had kissed and relieved of a tick during the pony's illness; he kills a "little thrush" with a slingshot, cuts it up because he is ashamed, and finally throws the parts away; and he asks his father, mother, and Billy about the large seaward mountains that suggest death to him in contrast with the "jolly" landward mountains, the Gabilans. The key to Jody's play is his fascination with death. Having become aware of it, he must understand its human meaning. He poses "the possibility of ancient cities lost in the mountains" to justify his deeper fascination. "Ancient cities" is an impossible fantasy, but the mountains become even more suggestive to Jody as a strictly private image; they are "dear to him, and terrible" in their mystery. Jody's secret fascination is drawn to one imagistic point by the appearance of Gitano, an old paisano, who comes back to his birthplace to die. After learning that the family adobe hut has washed away, and after staying a day and night with the Tiflins, Gitano travels into the great mountains that rim the Pacific, and he takes the old, useless horse, Easter; for the journey is to death.

All of this is a little too contrived. Nonetheless, it is made clear that Jody's mind works as a child's mind often does, through symbols in its preoccupation. That explains why Jody is so excited when Gitano appears. Jody can sense the painful reality of Gitano's wish to die, having learned about death in his own right, and he feels a kinship because he senses that Gitano's thoughts are like his own. Jody feels "irresistibly drawn" to the bunkhouse where Gitano is put up, since, in Jody's mind, Gitano's wish to die is associated with the seaward mountains. Indirectly but clearly, the narrative moves forward in a subsequent action, a fusion of the question that death raises with the theme of fatherhood. Jody finds Gitano with a rapier, and Gitano's initial anger at being spied on is changed to sympathy as he realizes the boy's need: "Jody put out his hand, 'Can't I see it?' Gitano's eyes smouldered angrily and he shook his head. 'Where'd you get it? Where'd it come from?' Now Gitano regarded him profoundly, as though he pondered. 'I got it from my father.'" Jody understands in turn that Gitano's reply is a sudden insight—the end of his search for a place to die. The privacy of the insight is shared in the objective fact of the rapier: "Jody knew . . . he must never tell anyone about the rapier. It would be a dreadful thing to tell anyone about it, for it would destroy some fragile structure of truth. It was a truth that might be shattered by division." The truth seems to be that death is only a natural fact, and it is natural because it is really a search for origins, for one's father. It is quite to the point that Jody's earlier eager questioning about treasure cities in the mountains forces Gitano to understand that his own search is really for a place to die that is his father's; for, as Jody questions, Gitano remembers that his father had taken him into the mountains once when he was a boy, and he comes to feel that only the mountains belong now to his father. This range of insight is not limited to the supporting phallic symbolism (mountains, rapier), or to the socially apt suggestion that Mr. Tiflin is not a warm father (a real father?) to Jody, or to the religious implications of "father," although all of these elements are relevant to the fragile structure of truth, which cannot be expressed simply.

THE CLIMAX, THOUGH CONTRIVED, CONVEYS JODY'S SORROW

Steinbeck is perhaps too simple at the climax of the episode, in the report the next morning that a neighbor has seen Gitano going into the seaward mountains, leading Easter and carrying a sword. Until that moment, the episode is developed surely.

Gitano's father contrasts sharply with Carl Tiflin. Gitano's father was a great man and was loved by his son, but Carl Tiflin is a fool. Interestingly, Steinbeck uses a version of his later allegorical method at its worst to suggest Mr. Tiflin's inability to sense that Gitano wishes to die. Mr. Tiflin is afraid of having to support the old man, and parallels him with Easter in a bad associative joke, suggestive of narrow stupidity, although Mr. Tiflin likes the joke so much (it *is* typical of him) that he repeats it: "Jody's father had a humorous thought. He turned to Gitano. 'If ham and eggs grew on a side-hill I'd turn you out to pasture too,' he said. 'But I can't afford to pasture you in my kitchen.'" Having innocently set off this exchange, Jody listens. Later, in the scene in the bunkhouse, Gitano is given the insight that Jody lacks a father he can respect fully. Still later, Gitano senses Jody's feeling that the rapier is a secret. And, for Jody, keeping the secret means keeping it especially from his father. Jody's lack of a respected father is emphasized—by ironic reversal—when Gitano goes into the mountains to find a place he can associate with his father. These narrative details draw together at the close. Mr. Tiflin thinks that Gitano has robbed him by taking Easter, but, with a deeper understanding, Jody walks out alone to look at the great mountains and to think about Gitano: "He lay down in the green grass . . . covered his eyes with his crossed arms . . . and he was full of a nameless sorrow." Jody's sorrow is for Gitano, for his probable death, and for the mystery of it. Even more, it is the sorrow of self-discovery, that imperfection is worse than death. Thus, Jody passes from a fascination with death, even from an older sorrow for the death of the red pony, to the profounder sorrow of recognizing that his father's limitations create or reveal imperfection at such close hand.

Clearly this episode is superior narrative work. Its relative inferiority to the surrounding episodes is due to some narrative strain. Mr. Tiflin's lack of sensibility is a much smaller point than the reality of death, and Mr. Tiflin's jovial stupidity cannot be elevated into a perfect correlation with Gitano's passion for his father. And the parallel between Gitano and Easter is much too self-conscious and slick in its surface emphasis. These imperfections keep "The Great Mountains" from attaining a thorough organic unity. The strength of the episode is in its success as an interlude, and its somewhat mechanical quality may have been intended precisely to relax the narrative tension to some extent. Certainly it occupies the mid-position between two very intense episodes. Finally, there is a thorough success in Steinbeck's transfer of Jody's awareness of death from the animal to the human sphere.

The Complex Life Game Involving Joy, Violence, Death, and Creation

The third episode, "The Promise," is absolutely an organic unity. It is one of Steinbeck's most impressive works. "The Promise" opens with a series of games that Jody plays by himself on the way from school. The games modulate from pure fantasy into the real world, from leadership of "a phantom army with great flags and swords, silent but deadly," through a batch of small animals that Jody stores, "moist and uncomfortable" in his lunch pail, to his eager collection of the mail from the box in front of the ranch, and finally to his mother's news that his father wants to see him. Here the real world intrudes clearly, and the game becomes adult—a game of creation that is "silent but deadly," that involves pain, yet more new experience than a weekly paper or a mail catalog can provide.

Mr. Tiflin has been convinced by Billy Buck that one of the ranch mares, Nellie, should be bred; her colt will replace the red pony. Mr. Tiflin masks the idea with a typical coldness; his offer is based on Jody's previous good behavior, and his condition is that Jody must earn the five-dollar stud fee by work around the ranch. Jody's response is a joyful fearfulness and respect for the stern father, and "a sudden warm friendliness" for Billy Buck as he realizes that the idea is Billy's. A forward movement containing the emotional content of the earlier episodes is clear now: Billy becomes Jody's substitute father, and Mr. Tiflin is allowed only a minimal role. Billy's stake is that he loves Jody as a father might; his benevolent idea is to let Jody help to create the new pony in the sense of helping at the birth of Nellie's colt. Mr. Tiflin's love is more objective and abstract. It is rooted in the virtue of duty and the value of money. So the idea is enmeshed from the beginning in Mr. Tiflin's private imperfections as a father and as a man.

Events deepen this suggestion. Jody brings Nellie to a neighbor who has a stallion; imagery controls the result:

> The stallion came on so fast that he couldn't stop when he reached the mare. Nellie's ears went back; she whirled and kicked at him as he went by. The stallion spun around and reared. He struck the mare with his front hoof, and while she staggered under the blow, his teeth raked her neck and drew an ooze of blood. Instantly, Nellie's mood changed. She became coquettishly feminine. . . . Jess Taylor sat the boy behind him on the horse. "You might have got killed," he said. "Sundown's a mean devil sometimes. He busted his rope and went right through a gate."

Nellie's mild injury, Jody's very probable danger, and the natural violence of the breeding, all presented from Jody's point of view, engender a train of imagery suggesting that violence, joy, and the chance of death are involved in creation—in an event more complex than a stud fee would imply through its reduction of the event to a calculated price. Mr. Tiflin, and Jody through him, tends to deny this complexity in the rationality of work. Jody's grinding schedule, set by Mr. Tiflin, repays the stud fee and pays for Nellie's special diet. As metaphor, father and son presume the colt's life has been paid for beforehand, hence assured, and Jody is his father's son to the extent that he expects the rational bargain to be kept.

But at birth the colt is twisted around in the womb; Billy has to kill Nellie to save the colt. Thus human and natural imperfection continue, and death remains the price of life.

The episode reaches a tragic plane, a heightening of the irony that we cannot buy a life, through Jody's shared awareness of Billy's suffering. Billy does what is "right" because he is determined to keep his promise to give Jody a colt, and he knows the mare has to die if the colt is to live. "Right" as it is, Billy's act is as bad, in effect, as the fact of a buzzard's endless hunger. Billy knows this; therefore he is stricken with guilt. A buzzard feels no guilt, nor does a man as unsubtle as Mr. Tiflin. The forward narrative movement from the first episode is in Billy's tragic awareness that the best he can do is imperfect, and Jody is able to comprehend this scale of moral awareness because it echoes his own earlier experience. Thus the narrative movement is completely organic and self-contained.

STEINBECK RETAINS JODY'S POINT OF VIEW THROUGHOUT

Steinbeck is very careful about this. Jody's point of view remains constant; it is through his essentially innocent perception that we realize the depth of Billy's sense of guilt. Always Jody's understanding is the center of the action, not the violence of birth in its bloody detail. And Jody's point of view is justified. He tends to substitute Billy Buck for his father, as human warmth for inhumanly chilly abstraction, but that does not lull his conviction that Billy is a fallible man. Hence, Jody wants to be certain that everything goes well. He makes Billy promise "you won't let anything happen" to the colt, and he insists on attending the birth. The price that Jody pays is a vision of Billy's self-torment. Billy's strain as the birth develops badly is established through his increasingly violent way of speaking to Jody. In the final sentence,

Jody's concentration on having the colt he has paid for and arranged to have is shifted completely under these influences to Jody's awareness of Billy's torment: "He tried to be glad because of the colt, but the bloody face, and the haunted, tired eyes of Billy Buck hung in the air ahead of him." So, fusing natural imperfection, death, and fatherhood, the episode ends in a human environment that is more significant than the colt, given Jody's established point of view. Human relevance is at one with the clarity of the narrative.

Like "The Gift," "The Promise" is an organic whole. Its events and characters imply a larger meaning that is implicit without strain in the narrative. There are no purely mechanical links, as there are in "The Great Mountains." Certain mechanical connections are evident, as in "The Gift," but they remain minor details that only tighten the events. Thus, Jess Taylor, who saw Gitano going away, owns the stallion in "The Promise." Jody's colt is intended to replace the red pony. A year passes and Jody thinks he will be too old before he can ride the new colt. In fact, he is growing mature enough to comprehend tragedy, not merely death. The major themes are always kept in view and focus the organic development of the narrative. In brief, details are not ends in themselves; they support the whole.

Clearly, then, *The Red Pony* can stand with *In Dubious Battle,* much of *The Grapes of Wrath,* and *The Pearl* as among Steinbeck's most impressive successes in the art of narrative.

Structural Patterns Unify *The Red Pony*

John H. Timmerman

John H. Timmerman analyzes patterns that unify *The Red Pony.* In particular, he claims that Jody's rebellion against his father, the recurrence of visions and dreams, and the progress of Jody's maturation tie all the stories together. John H. Timmerman teaches English at Calvin College in Grand Rapids, Michigan. He is the author of *John Steinbeck's Fiction: The Aesthetics of the Road Taken, Other Worlds: The Fantasy Genre,* and "John Steinbeck's Use of the Bible: A Descriptive Bibliography of the Critical Tradition" in *Steinbeck Quarterly.*

While standing independently of each other, the *Red Pony* stories share an organic structural unity as a whole through several patterns. The first of these is a natural time progression beginning in Jody's tenth year and ending in his twelfth. "The Gift" begins in late August, with the start of the school year, and concludes with Gabilan's death shortly before Thanksgiving, at the start of the rainy winter season. "The Great Mountains" begins in midsummer of the following year, and the entire story covers less than twenty-four hours. The rage that Jody vents at the end of "The Gift" by smashing a buzzard's head carries over to the beginning of "The Great Mountains," when he kills a thrush with a stone and cuts off the bird's head. "The Gift" ends with Jody smeared with the blood from the buzzard; in "The Great Mountains," Jody "drank from the mossy tub and washed the bird's blood from his hands in cold water."

THE STRUCTURE OF SEASONS AND DAYS AND YOUTH

"The Promise" begins in the spring of the following year and ends on February 2 with the death of Nellie and the birth of the black colt. "The Leader of the People" begins in the spring, when Billy Buck rakes together "the last of the old year's haystack." The stories, then, follow an annual cycle, covering events in two years of the life of Jody Tiflin.

Other subtle patterns lend a structured unity to the whole. While the first story begins at daybreak, suggesting the youth and innocence of Jody, subsequent stories begin on "a midsummer afternoon," "mid-afternoon of spring," and a "Saturday afternoon." The rhythmical pattern may be extended, as [critic] Arnold L. Goldsmith observes in "Thematic Rhythm in *The Red Pony*": "Steinbeck follows the violence of the first story with the tragic quiet of the second, with this same pattern repeated in the third and fourth sections. Where the first and third stories are about the violent deaths of horses, the second and fourth are about the twilight years of two old men." The entire pattern, Goldsmith points out, represents "the neverending rhythm of life and death to which Jody is continually exposed."

Throughout the cycle of changes, however, Steinbeck persistently identifies Jody, at the beginning of each story, as a youth. In "The Gift" we meet him as "only a little boy, ten years old, with hair like yellow grass and with shy polite gray eyes, and with a mouth that worked when he thought." In subsequent stories he is introduced each time as "the little boy Jody." Thus the larger theme emerges: A little boy is finding his place in the larger rhythmical patterns of life and death, of passing time, of dreams and responsibilities.

Steinbeck made his thematic intentions for *The Red Pony* quite clear. In addition to the notes and letters of the time, we have a remarkably candid retrospective statement in "My Short Novels":

> *The Red Pony* was written a long time ago, when there was desolation in my family. The first death occurred. And the family which every child believes to be immortal, was shattered. Perhaps this is the first adulthood of any man or woman. The first tortured question "Why?" and then acceptance, and then the child becomes a man. *The Red Pony* was as attempt, an experiment if you wish, to set down this loss and acceptance and growth.

The pattern of "loss and acceptance and growth" furnishes the basic theme for the tales and culminates very successfully in the much-disputed "The Leader of the People."

THE PATTERN OF JODY'S REBELLION AGAINST CARL

The maturation of Jody is developed in several minor patterns that complement and sustain the major pattern of the experience of death. The most notable of these is the relationship with his father, Carl. From the start Carl Tiflin demonstrates three qualities that provide a framework for Jody's adolescent spirit of rebellion: stern discipline, incipient cruelty, and pragmatic realism.

A stern, unbending man, Carl possesses a rigid sense of ordered discipline. This is all that Jody has known—an unyielding framework of rules. He obeys his father "in everything without questions of any kind." Rules are produced by Carl with the aim of order, but also of training Jody to his high sense of dignity. Thus, he suspects Jody's own careful training of Gabilan because it might produce a "trick horse." Watching Gabilan working on the long halter, Carl observes, "He's getting to be almost a trick pony. . . . I don't like trick horses. It takes all the—dignity out of a horse to make him do tricks. Why, a trick horse is kind of like an actor—no dignity, no character of his own." What Carl fails to see is the association between Gabilan's training and his own training of Jody. It has never occurred to him that his own rigid discipline threatens Jody's independence, almost transforming him into a trick boy. So it is also that Jody's sense of revolt at Carl's rules becomes closely allied with Gabilan's spirit, for Jody is very much a young boy in rebellion, finding his own ways to assert his independence. Walking through the vegetable garden, "He paused for a moment to smash a green muskmelon with his heel, but he was not happy about it. It was a bad thing to do, he knew perfectly well." This minor act of defiance is a part of the general rebellion at the start of the school year: "There was still a spirit of revolt among the pupils." Jody's independent spirit is mirrored in Gabilan, whose eyes shine with "the light of disobedience."

Carl's character is marked by a kind of aloof and stern dignity, but be can also be a cruel man. His incipient cruelty is openly manifested with old Gitano. While hating the brutality he shows to Gitano, he nonetheless turns on the old man:

> "It's a shame not to shoot Easter," he said. "It'd save him a lot of pains and rheumatism." He looked secretly at Gitano, to see whether he noticed the parallel, but the big bony hands did not move, nor did the dark eyes turn from the horse. "Old things ought to be put out of their misery," Jody's father went on. "One shot, a big noise, one big pain in the head maybe, and that's all. That's better than stiffness and sore teeth."

The cruelty carries to Grandfather as well, for here too is an "old thing" that ought to be put out of his misery. Ironically,

Carl's own cruelty defeats him. Thinking that Grandfather is out of earshot, Carl berates the old man mercilessly. Terribly shamed by his outburst, Carl stalks out of the kitchen, but Jody has witnessed the unraveling of his father's stern dignity:

> Jody glanced in shame at his mother, and he saw that she was looking at Carl, and that she wasn't breathing. It was an awful thing that he was doing. He was tearing himself to pieces to talk like that. It was a terrible thing to him to retract a word, but to retract it in shame was infinitely worse.

The tyrannical order of sternness has crumbled, and in its wreckage Jody comes of age. With his father's harshness shattered by shame, and bearing in mind Carl's attitude toward "old things" as worthless clutter, Jody steps into the role that rightfully should be Carl's. Having lost heart for the gratuitous violence of killing the mice in the haystack, Jody ushers Grandfather into the house and makes him a glass of lemonade, the right action toward an old thing whose only sin has been to run out of room for his great dream of westering. Jody becomes the leader of the party.

To describe Carl Tiflin in such a way is not to imply that he is a mean or malicious man. Indeed, many readers have assumed that because he is the foil for Jody's maturation and for the key role-reversal in "The Leader of the People," Carl is something of the villain in the story. Billy Buck, in this view, operates as surrogate father to the boy, providing nurture and understanding. It would be more accurate, however, to characterize Carl as a victim of his own pragmatic concerns. Twice before the climactic shaming before Grandfather, he has his own attempts at capturing some larger vision thwarted. When Gabilan is dying, Carl attempts to cheer Jody by telling stories:

> He told about the wild man who ran naked through the country and had a tail and ears like a horse and he told about the rabbit-cats of Moro Cojo that hopped into the trees for birds. He revived the famous Maxwell brothers who found a vein of gold and hid the traces of it so carefully that they could never find it again.

Asking for some response from the silent, withdrawn Jody, Carl reacts with hurt and anger. He has no other resources. The scene foreshadows "The Leader of the People," wherein Carl himself ignores Grandfather's stories.

In "The Great Mountains," after cruelly demeaning Gitano, Carl again feels remorse: "Jody sat and secretly watched his father. He knew how mean his father felt." In this instance, Carl has failed to participate in Gitano's vision of a transcendent power in life, again foreshadowing his reaction to Grandfather. Stern he may be, even cruel at times, but Carl Tiflin represents nothing quite so much as a pragmatic authority locked in a prison of his own making.

JODY'S REBELLION RESOLVED IN THE LAST STORY

"The Leader of the People," which brings the conflict between Jody and Carl to a culmination, gave Steinbeck considerably more difficulty than the other *Red Pony* stories. He seemed to want a sense of closure to the tales and to the thematic pattern of Jody's revolt and Carl's sternness. In an early draft the focus of the conflict centered upon the haystack, which served as an omen of tragedy:

> From the very first the haystack in the lower field was ill fated. In July when the pole was set up and the loaded header had creaked up beside it, the big Jackson fork slipped and drove a tine through Billy Buck's foot. The little boy Jody watched Billy pull off his shoe and pour blood out of it, and jerk off his sock to prevent the poisoning of black dye. Billy was laid up then. Jody himself led the horse that pulled the Jackson fork tackle. At last the tall yellow stack was made and Jody's father thatched it carefully to keep the rain water out. That very afternoon Jody slid down the stack a few times and ruined the thatching so that it had to be done over again. This piece of badness on Jody's part not only brought instant punishment but had a far-reaching and sharp effect on the following Christmas, for Jody's father Carl Tiflin was an irreparable punisher and keeper of his threats.

The scene sets a conflict between Carl and Jody Tiflin, but it also depicts Jody as still a very immature child, rambunctious to be sure, but also willfully destructive for his own pleasure. It lacks the sense of growth Steinbeck had been aiming at.

In a second start to the story, under the title of "Grandfather," Steinbeck begins with Jody's being punished in school for shooting a needle through a reed blowgun into the woodwork around the blackboard. The teacher treats the offense promptly, but with a certain degree of lightness. This scene leads into the revised haystack scene, in which Carl catches him sliding down the haystack: "This piece of badness not only brought an instant punishment but had a far-reaching effect on the following Christmas, for Jody's father Carl Tiflin was a stern punisher and a keeper of his threats." The same conflict is there, and we never do learn the effect on the following Christmas. In this version, however, Jody vents his anger at being punished upon the mice in the haystack: "Those sleek, fat, smug mice who had lived all winter in the warm hay stack were good objects of revenge for all the evil of the stack. And Billy Buck had said the moldy straw was fairly crawling with fat frightened mice. Jody licked his nervous lips."

The mice hunt, which had appeared in bits and pieces throughout the ledger, exists in the final version only as a great expectancy. But when the moment arrives, right after Carl's shame, Jody doesn't feel the same vengeful urge. Instead he gives up the hunt to wait upon Grandfather. Rebellion and vengeance are thereby replaced by a loving act of service. The full significance of Jody's bestowal of an act of grace upon Grandfather, however, is revealed in Jody's knowledge of death and Grandfather's great dream of westering, a pattern carefully and artistically developed in the work.

THE PATTERN OF DETAILS IN SETTING AND CHARACTER

If, as Steinbeck so often commented, the *Red Pony* stories were an escape from the pressing reality of his mother's illness, the artistic discipline marking these stories is the more remarkable. The tales contain some of Steinbeck's finest, most carefully controlled descriptive passages to date, especially in the detailed portrayal of setting. The landscape of the Tiflin ranch emerges in crisply detailed portraits, seen by impressionistic snatches through Jody's eyes:

> On the fences the shiny blackbirds with red epaulets clicked their dry call. The meadowlarks sang like water, and the wild doves, concealed among the bursting leaves of the oaks, made a sound of restrained grieving. In the fields the rabbits sat sunning themselves, with only their forked ears showing above the grass heads.

Steinbeck is not so much inventing as remembering in such passages; these are his foothills. Such descriptions rivet the landscape in sterling portraits.

The same use of intimate details characterizes Jody and make his youthfulness believable. The boy isn't precious; indeed, his humanity is seen in his relentless mistreatment of the enduring Doubletree Mutt, as fine a character as has limped through any of Steinbeck's stories and a testament to his lifelong affection for dogs. In a sense, Doubletree serves as the convenient displacement for Jody's revolt under his father's rules. But Jody isn't a mean sort; his world is an imaginative, if sometimes lonely, one:

> Banging his knee against the golden lard bucket he used for
> school lunch, he contrived a good bass drum, while his
> tongue fluttered sharply against his teeth to fill in snare
> drums and occasional trumpets. Some time back the other
> members of the squad that walked so smartly from the school
> had turned into the various little canyons and taken the
> wagon roads to their own home ranches. Now Jody marched
> seemingly alone, with high-lifted knees and pounding feet;
> but behind him there was a phantom army with great flags
> and swords, silent but deadly.

In such portraits, Steinbeck reveals the imaginative quality of
Jody that makes him more receptive to the mysteriousness of
death and that opposes him to Carl's pragmatic rigidity.

In addition to his precise descriptions of a boy's world and
his ability to capture Jody's youthful spirit, Steinbeck admits
us to Jody's world through the eyes of others. News of Gabilan's arrival infects the schoolhouse boys with wonder, and
Jody suddenly appears huge and marvelous before their eyes:

> Before today Jody had been a boy, dressed in overalls and a
> blue shirt—quieter than most, even suspected of being a little
> cowardly. And now he was different. Out of a thousand cen-
> turies they drew the ancient admiration of the footman for
> the horseman. They knew instinctively that a man on a horse
> is spiritually as well as physically bigger than a man on foot.
> They knew that Jody had been miraculously lifted out of
> equality with them, and had been placed over them.

While the boys traipse home in awestruck wonder, it is Jody
who is left with the work of currying and brushing Gabilan.
His wonder is vested in the pony itself.

The care of horses leads also to the care of Grandfather.
On the one hand, this care of Gabilan and then Nellie results
from Carl's dictates. Carl, who believes it is good discipline
to give presents with reservations, adjures Jody to care for
Gabilan: "If I ever hear of you not feeding him or leaving his
stall dirty, I'll sell him off in a minute." When he decides to
breed Nellie, once again Carl admonishes Jody: "You'll have
to take care of her, too, till she throws the colt." But Carl's
"care" is the rigid code of discipline unaffected by the emotions of the heart. Precisely those stirrings of the heart lead
Jody to care for Grandfather after Carl shames him.

THE STRUCTURE OF VISIONARY DREAMS

Jody is also touched by a sense of the mystical dream that
places him closer to Grandfather's vision of westering than
Carl. Carl's line of imagination seldom stretches beyond his

own land, possibly as far as a sale in Salinas. He is the harsh, pragmatic man, incapable of dreaming. While less successful as a farmer, he is a bit like Raymond Banks, incapable of an imaginative world, and therefore impatient with Grandfather's great vision of westering. But from the outset, Jody has a keen sense of the transcendent vision.

Three great visionary dreams appear in the sequence of the tales, united by the mystical lure of the mountains and threading together the boy Jody, the dying Gitano, and the aged Grandfather. Each of them senses, in his own way, the power in life that transcends pragmatic reality, even mortality. One line of maturation in Jody is in the deepening sensitivity toward and appreciation for that mystical sense.

In "The Gift" Jody has fears for the welfare of his colt, the kind of childish nightmares that persist even into the waking vision. But these fears are described by Steinbeck as "a strong and a mysterious journey, to Jody—an extension of a dream." At this point he has no personal experience of life and death, simply feeling its dialectic as a raw possibility, a gray threat. At the end of the story, with Gabilan ill, Jody's sleep is disrupted as "the breathy groans of the pony sounded in his dreams." It is after the death of Gabilan, at the beginning of "The Great Mountains," that Jody first senses the mystical transcendence of vision, rather than merely dreaming. Lying on his back on a hill, Jody seems lifted toward the mountains. He squints his eyes, varying perspective. In a passage reminiscent of Gertie in "Fingers of Cloud," Steinbeck describes the experience:

> By closing one eye and destroying perspective he brought them down within reach so that he could put up his fingers and stroke them. He helped the gentle wind push them down the sky; it seemed to him that they went faster for his help. One fat white cloud he helped clear to the mountain rims and pressed it firmly over, out of sight. Jody wondered what it was seeing, then. He sat up the better to look at the great mountains where they went piling back, growing darker and more savage until they finished with one jagged ridge, high up against the west. Curious secret mountains; he thought of the little he knew about them.

The vision sets up the dialectic of the great mountains in the story, this geographical antithesis between the bright, mystical Gabilans and the darker, foreboding Santa Lucia range. Jody feels the mystic pull of the life-holding Gabilans: "They were jolly mountains, with hill ranches in their creases, and with pine trees growing on the crests." He fears the western Santa Lucia range with its strange, dark pull upon his spirit: "In the evening . . . the mountains were a purple-like despair, then Jody was afraid of them; then they were so impersonal and aloof that their very imperturbability was a threat." The paired ranges operate metaphorically here, as they would often in Steinbeck's work. In *East of Eden*, he recollects his own experience of the mountains in words that echo *The Red Pony*:

> I remember that the Gabilan Mountains to the east of the valley were light gay mountains full of sun and loveliness and a kind of invitation, so that you wanted to climb into the lap of a beloved mother. They were beckoning mountains with a brown grass love. The Santa Lucias stood up against the sky to the west and kept the valley from the open sea, and they were dark and brooding—unfriendly and dangerous. I always found in myself a dread of west and a love of east.

Jody finds himself juxtaposed between, puzzled by, and finding his way through the contrary pulls of light and dark, life and death.

Having experienced the terror of death in Gabilan, Jody is tutored in the meaning of death and mystical transcendence by old Gitano: "Gitano was mysterious like the mountains. There were ranges back as far as you could see, but behind the last range piled up against the sky there was a great unknown country. And Gitano was an old man, until you got to the dull dark eyes. And in behind them was some unknown thing." When Jody had asked Carl what lay beyond the mountains, Carl answered in pragmatic terms: more mountains, cliffs, and brush and rocks and dryness, at last the ocean. But "Jody knew something was there, something very wonderful because it wasn't known, something secret and mysterious. He could feel within himself that this was so." That sense of the mysterious, the unknown, is unlocked by old Gitano. But when Jody presses Gitano for answers, Gitano simply refuses to tell him. The discovery of mystical transcendence, of a power that lies beyond human understanding, is finally one that each person makes individually.

The questing mind and the deep sensitivity to the transcendent dream admit Jody more fully than any other family member to Grandfather's vision of westering. To the others his tales are just old stories, repeated too often in the fashion of the elderly who have outlived their time and vaguely irritating because they divert attention from pragmatic realities. Grandfather has had his place in the sun, but the sun is declining on the wall of the Tiflin kitchen. Does it matter to Carl how he got this farm, when all of his concern is for its present demands? Does the dream of new possibilities have any influence over actions at this place, actions ruled by responsibilities rather than possibilities? For Carl the answer is adamantly no. But Jody's mind is of a different cast. He has sensed the vision of the transcendent power of a larger dream in old Gitano. Furthermore, he has witnessed the death of his beloved colt, but also the birth of a new colt from the death of Nellie. Intuitively, he has arrived at a deep sensitivity to new life arising from the passing of the old, but also the congruence of the old and new. This hunger for life is raw in him and is nurtured by Grandfather's vision of westering.

The westering concept has been the subject of considerable debate by Steinbeck scholars. Seen by some simply as an old man's maudlin and rambling recollection, it appears to be a flaw in the pattern of the tales. Seen by others as an adumbration of Steinbeck's phalanx theory[1]—which it most certainly is—some have failed to see its close tie to the maturation of Jody and his growing vision of life and death. Grandfather doesn't simply lament the loss of leadership; he laments the loss of the vision that he calls "westering." Life has been reduced to the routine; the dream has disappeared. But Jody has experienced the dream. The legacy of westering now lives in him. The passing of the dream from old hands to new is signified by Jody's serving Grandfather the lemonade. Jody relinquishes the mouse hunt, something he has looked forward to for days and something entirely self-serving, in order to cheer up Grandfather. His selfless compassion marks him, in Grandfather's own terms, as the leader of the people who served others before himself. [Critic] Robert Morsberger observes, "'Westering' may be dead in subdivisions" in today's world, but Steinbeck demonstrates in *The Red Pony* that the dream does indeed live on that it may be handed from one generation to the next. Jody's maturation in the stories is, finally, the inheritance of the great vision.

Jody's maturation into knowledge of life and death and

---

1. The theory that group-man, made up of many people, has a will and direction of its own.

his appropriation of Grandfather's great dream of westering do not absolve all conflict, however. It would be more precise to say that he now holds life and death in tension, rather than to say that he sees a transcendent vision of a life force that abnegates death. The latter might be said about Joseph Wayne of *To a God Unknown*, who even while dying feels the rejuvenative surge of rain upon him. The tension develops, possibly, not out of Steinbeck's mystical attraction evidenced in Joseph Wayne, but out of his practical experience of the illness of his mother.

THE STRUCTURE OF TENSION

That tension is supplied in several ways in the stories. Billy Buck, whom Jody reveres above all men, finding in him a wisdom born of experience that transcends his father's sternness, is at once a life-bringer and executioner. He must smash Nellie's skull before bringing forth the colt, an action that also tears Billy apart for, as he says, "I'm half horse myself, you see." At the end of "The Promise," Billy Buck bears the blood from Nellie like a wound on his own face. It is that wound that Jody remembers, and the look of despair on Billy's face.

The tension is also supplied in the juxtaposed symbols of the cypress tree and the watering pipe. Frequently Jody wanders between these two places, always feeling a cold dread of the cypress tree and a warm sympathy for the watering place. The two places develop symbolically throughout the stories in direct intensity and proportion to Jody's own understanding of the life-death tension.

In "The Gift" the two are matter-of-factly introduced as physical places on the farm. While drinking from the trough by the spring, Jody can glance downhill and see the cypress:

> He leaned over and drank close to the green mossy wood where the water tasted best. Then he turned and looked back on the ranch, on the low, whitewashed house girded with red geraniums, and on the long bunkhouse by the cypress tree where Billy Buck lived alone. Jody could see the great black kettle under the cypress tree. That was where the pigs were scalded.

The cypress, traditional symbol of death and a feature of cemeteries, is immediately associated with death and loss. Having looked upon it, Jody feels "an uncertainty in the air, a feeling of change and of loss and of the gain of new and unfamiliar things." As if in response to the tremulous sense of fear, two black buzzards glide past.

The tension between cypress and watering place is emphasized when Gabilan becomes ill and Jody begins to sense the symbolism of the juxtaposition: "He looked down at the house and at the old bunkhouse and at the dark cypress tree. The place was familiar, but curiously changed. It wasn't itself any more, but a frame for things that were happening." Weighty and thick, the cypress hunkers like a perpetual shadow on the landscape of the story. The pellucid waters of the spring charge along a line of greenery to the watering trough where the animals nourish themselves. The pigs snuffle at the trough; behind them hangs the singletree and the black tub for slaughter.

In "The Great Mountains," where Jody's sense of life and death broadens from the experience of Gabilan to human experiences in old Gitano, the cypress-watering place symbolism intensifies. Having just killed the thrush, Jody washes himself at the trough. It cleanses and rejuvenates, but the cypress stands unyieldingly before him.

In "The Promise" the symbolism is made overt, paralleling Jody's own growth in understanding the tensions of life and death:

> The water whined softly into the trough all the year round. This place had grown to be a center-point for Jody. When he had been punished the cool green grass and the singing water soothed him. When he had been mean the biting acid of meanness left him at the brush line. When he sat in the grass and listened to the purling stream, the barriers set up in his mind by the stern day went down to ruin.

The trough is the "center-point," but the cypress is the counter-point:

> On the other hand, the black cypress tree by the bunkhouse was as repulsive as the water-tub was dear; for to this tree all the pigs came, sooner or later, to be slaughtered. Pig killing was fascinating, with the screaming and the blood, but it made Jody's heart beat so fast that it hurt him. After the pigs were scalded in the big iron tripod kettle and their skins were scraped and white, Jody had to go to the water-tub to sit in the grass until his heart grew quiet. The water-tub and the black cypress were opposites and enemies.

Immediately Jody associates the opposition with Nellie and the unborn colt, Black Demon. The trilling water nurtures his dream for the colt, but he cannot escape the presence of the cypress. As Jody walks into the barn when Nellie is due, he walks through a blackness in which only the cypress stands out, a darker blackness against the night.

DEATH, LIFE, AND TRUTH—THEMES OF JODY'S MATURING

Neither the tree nor the trough appears in "The Leader of the People." The symbolism is manifested in life itself with the appearance of Grandfather. This time, Billy Buck states the tension as Jody prepares to attack the mice in the haystack:

> Jody changed his course and moved toward the house. He leaned his flail against the steps. "That's to drive the mice out," he said. "I'll bet they're fat. I'll bet they don't know what's going to happen to them today."
>
> "No, nor you either," Billy remarked philosophically. "Nor me, nor anyone."
>
> Jody was staggered by this thought. He knew it was true. His imagination twitched away from the mouse hunt.

Here the tension is stated overtly: Death and life hang in a delicate balance. This too has been Jody's discovery in the course of his maturation.

[Writer and critic] Lev Shestov, writing on the conflict between reason and revelation in his major work *Athens and Jerusalem*, argues that our present age is trapped in the cold hands of pragmatic necessity. His essential question might serve as a coda for *The Red Pony*:

> Is it given men to judge the truths, to decide the fate of the truths? On the contrary, it is the truths which judge men and decide their fate and not men who rule over the truths. Men, the great as well as the small, are born and die, appear and disappear—but the truth remains.

Jody senses the truth in a way that Carl Tiflin will never approach. From the "little boy Jody," checked constantly by his father's discipline, dignity, and occasional cruelty, he has matured not necessarily to adult wisdom but to a sense of fullness of life that holds living and dying, reality and the dream, in balance. The passage has required loss and desolation, but it has produced the tempered steel of actions of the heart.

Against a backdrop of enervating personal turmoil, *The Red Pony* represents an artistic triumph for Steinbeck. The carefully paced theme of maturity through the desolation of loss, and the heightened sense of a transcendent vision that rises above the narrowness of pragmatic reality, carry the weight of a deeply meaningful work. The artistic craftsmanship, the carefully plotted patterns of description, symbolism, and imagery, carry the energy of an intriguing and moving story. It is an enduring work, a classic by virtue of its profound simplicity, unswervingly faithful in capturing the childhood point of view, disciplined in its narration.

Moreover, in the development of his fictional artistry, the sequence of stories represents a liberation for Steinbeck. In them he moves to the heart of his artistic talent. It is a historical irony that he completed *The Pastures of Heaven* and *The Red Pony* while simultaneously revising *To a God Unknown,* for these separate works represent the dialectic of his fictional career: stories of personal experience and a recollected past versus a story of philosophical breadth and open-ended speculation. Finding now some scant degree of commercial success with the former—as much as the whimsical wrath of the Great Depression would allow—Steinbeck felt a degree of benediction upon the kind of story he wanted to tell, the stories of *his* heart. A path opened for him in *The Red Pony* that would be well traveled in future years.

Steinbeck's Mature Style in *The Red Pony*

Harry Thornton Moore

Harry Thornton Moore claims that John Steinbeck's early writing in *The Red Pony* is mature. In this partly autobiographical story, Steinbeck's style succeeds both in his creation of characters and his glowing depiction of ranch life in the Salinas Valley. These stories tell about Jody's first exposure to birth and death, hard experiences that initiate him into the realities of life. Harry Thornton Moore taught English at Northwestern University, Evanston, Illinois, and Southern Illinois University, Carbondale. He is the author of *The Life and Works of D.H. Lawrence*, *E.M. Forster*, and *Henry James and His World*.

Between the publication dates of *To A God Unknown* [1933], which demarcated the end of Steinbeck's first period as a writer, and those of that very different first book of his next phase, *Tortilla Flat* [1935], there was a gap of more than a year and a half. During this interval (indeed, soon after the appearance of *To A God Unknown*) the first two parts of the short-story group later called *The Red Pony* were printed in the lone magazine which would accept Steinbeck's work at this time, *The North American Review*. Four years later, in 1937, the whole of *The Red Pony* was issued in book form in a limited edition; it was given to the wide public a year after that in the first collected volume of Steinbeck's short stories [*The Long Valley*]. The important point to remember is that *The Red Pony* is an early work, though it may seem otherwise because of its late appearance in book form and because its straightforward observation and its sense of control make its writing resemble the later books.

Excerpted from Harry Thornton Moore, *The Novels of John Steinbeck: A First Critical Study* (Chicago: Normandie House, 1939). Reprinted by permission of the Estate of Harry Thornton Moore.

A NEW ELEMENT IN STEINBECK'S WRITING

The Red Pony tells the story of "the boy Jody," obviously a partly autobiographical character, who is seen in relation to different phases of life at his father's ranch—the animals, the people, the surrounding country. The harshness of the world is always ready to make itself felt, but in the times between the descents of doom we again find the glow that seems to play over Steinbeck's work when he is writing of daily ranch-life. The story really comprises three stories: they concern the horrible death of a pony, the hard birth of a colt, and the return of an old *paisano* to the place where he had been born. This last-mentioned section is one of Steinbeck's finest stories, despite the too-obvious comparison of the weary old man with the spent old horse (a somewhat similar parallel was to be used with greater subtlety but no less trickery in *Of Mice and Men*). Yet the other parts of this story, "The Great Mountains," are effective. And there is something new: Steinbeck deals with the concept of private property in a way he had never dealt with it before. The old *paisano*'s home had once been on the site of the present ranch, and when he was a boy he had lived there with his father, even as Jody is now dwelling there with his own father. The old man is first seen by Jody, to whom he says simply, "I am Gitano, and I have come back." Jody's mother and father try to get rid of Gitano, but he is as implacable as [American writer Herman] Melville's Bartleby. They think he is looking for work, but no, he is too old to work. "I will stay here until I die." But he is not permitted to stay, he is worth no more to Jody's father than the useless old horse. It was apparent that a new yeast was working in Steinbeck in his first story of the dispossessed.

The Red Pony contains some of the finest prose passages Steinbeck had yet written. There is for example this account of Jody rising early in the California morning and going out to see his new pony in the barn:

> In the grey quiet mornings when the land and the brush and the houses and the trees were silver-grey and black like a photograph negative, he stole toward the barn, past the sleeping stone and the sleeping cypress tree. The turkeys, roosting in the tree out of coyotes' reach, clicked drowsily. The fields glowed with a grey frost-like light and in the dew the tracks of rabbits and of field mice stood out sharply. The good dogs came stiffly out of their little houses, hackles up and deep growls in their throats. Then they caught Jody's scent and their stiff tails rose up and waved a greeting. . . .

STEINBECK'S LONG VALLEY

John Steinbeck grew up in the Salinas Valley, which lies near the Pacific coast in California and is the setting for all of the stories in The Red Pony. *In* The Novels of John Steinbeck: A First Critical Study, *Harry Thornton Moore identifies the valley's location and explains its importance in Steinbeck's life and writing.*

Salinas is ten miles inland from the notch Monterey Bay makes in the California Coast. The town was settled about 1858, and since 1872 has been the seat of Monterey County, of which John Steinbeck's father was treasurer for many years. Salinas lies near the north end of the "long valley" whose checkerboard farms produce lettuce, cauliflower, beets, fruit and grain in one of America's richest agricultural regions. To the east of the valley the Gabilan Mountains rise, hill ranches on the slopes, black-green belts of pinewoods, and—just above Soledad—Vancouver's Pinnacles thrusting up their spire-like rock formations. On the west the Santa Lucia range cuts off the Salinas Valley from the coast: the flanks of these mountains carry the burden of sequoia forests, there are great passes of broken granite, and fogs from the sea are often tangled in the pine-crested heights. . . .

John Ernst Steinbeck, Jr., was born at Salinas on February 27, 1902. He was the only boy in the family. One of his sisters, Esther, became a home-demonstration agent at Redding, in the northern part of the state, and another sister is Mrs. Carrol Rodgers of Watsonville, near Salinas. Both of the Steinbeck parents died several years ago.

A friend has described Steinbeck's home-life as having been "definitely bourgeois." He must have been a somewhat solemn child, judging from the temperament of "the boy Jody" in *The Red Pony*, who seems to be a partly autobiographical character. Steinbeck has remarked that children are wise rather than gay.

There was much to make life interesting for a boy in that region: readers of *The Red Pony* will recall how impressed Jody was with the mountains that lifted above him—the Gabilans were "jolly," but the mountains on the coast side seemed to have a menace. It is evident from all his writing how the fertile bed of the valley attracted Steinbeck; it was full of living and growing things, cattle and the fruit and grain and vegetables being raised and produced there.

Harry Thornton Moore, *The Novels of John Steinbeck: A First Critical Study.* Chicago: Normandie House, 1939.

The pictures here are superb, and the passage is improved by the break in the prevailing style made by the word "good," which may seem faintly out of key, though it is essentially so right, giving a touch of informality and warmth in just the proper place. It is the kind of risk a man who is writing good prose can afford to take.

A New Style in *The Red Pony*

Randolph Bartlett

Reviewing a special 1937 edition of *The Red Pony*, Randolph Bartlett emphasizes Steinbeck's new refined style, a style especially suited to the subtle themes portrayed in the three stories in this edition. Moreover, Bartlett praises the forcefulness of the work and obvious familiarity Steinbeck has with the setting, with horses, and with the psyche of a young boy. Randolph Bartlett is a journalist and book reviewer.

John Steinbeck, scrawling rowdy caricatures in charcoal on butcher's paper, has laid aside his familiar tools to prove his artistry with—of all things—the etcher's needle. There was never any doubt of his mastery of the other medium. He proved it in the boisterous and bawdy *Tortilla Flat* and the sinister and fleshly *Of Mice and Men*. It was not to be expected that he would be equally at home in a medium which requires finesse in place of brutality, and yet here is *The Red Pony*.

THREE SELF-CONTAINED NOVELETTES

This latest work consists of three novelettes, each self-contained and yet threaded in sequence, depicting the life of a boy on a ranch in that part of California Mr. Steinbeck knows so thoroughly, between the naive south and the sophisticated north, the Monterey region. Delicately, and affectionately, he reveals the very soul of the lad, his love for animals, his appreciation of generosity, his faith in his elders, his great need to do some violent thing when tragedy has shattered his hopes and dreams.

The first story tells of a gift from his father of a pony of his own, a pony he must teach to love and respect him, a pony to train and one day to ride. Lest it might be inferred that this

Reprinted from Randolph Bartlett, "Tang of Stage," in *John Steinbeck: The Contemporary Reviews*, edited by Joseph R. McElrath Jr., Jesse S. Crisler, and Susan Shillingsaw (New York: Cambridge University Press, 1996).

is a mere tale for boys it must be added that Mr. Steinbeck is equally effective in picturing the family background of his little hero, Jody. There is his father, a man of keen understanding and with all the wisdom of the ranges; his mother, stern but gentle, and quick to sense her son's needs; Billy Buck, the ranch hand, who knew all about horses that there was to know. It is a kindly atmosphere.

The second story, "The Great Mountains," deals with the return to the ranch of a man who had been born there, a Mexican, now grown old and asking only a place to sleep and a little food. This is an interlude between the other two novelettes, in which the boy fills in a void in his life by dreaming and inquiring about the mountains in the distance, what is to be found there, and what lies beyond.

The third story, "The Promise," carries the boy to the fulfillment of his wish, through doubts and apprehension which have crept into his consciousness because of the experiences through which he has gone in the two previous episodes. This time, a horse is to be bred for him, and at the end of the long period of waiting there occurs a denouement that is the one touch of the ruthless Steinbeck in the series.

STEINBECK'S REFINED STYLE

An interesting characteristic of this work is that in the transition from charcoal to stylus, Mr. Steinbeck has lost nothing of his force and vitality. He merely seems to have realized that in dealing with this essentially human narrative, it was necessary to adopt a different technic than was useful in picturing the denizens of Tortilla Flat or the men of violence in *Of Mice and Men.*

The effectiveness of his work is due in a very large measure to the fact that he obviously knows intimately the region of which he writes. The reader cannot fail to sense the tang of sage in the dusty air, nor to see the nodding bunches of wild oats on the hillside. Horses too he knows, inside and out, and what is going on in their minds, and boys he knows and must love, or he could not have written of Jody as he did.

It must be assumed that there will be subsequent editions of this charming work. The present format is exquisite, a large paper edition with a flexible linen cover, and limited to 699 copies, as if [publishers] Covici-Friede were anxious to accentuate the difference between the old Steinbeck and the new. The picture is entirely worthy of its luxurious frame.

Steinbeck Praised as a Short-Story Writer

Jay Parini

Biographer Jay Parini recounts critical praise given *The Long Valley* when it was published in 1938. According to Parini, the theme of *The Red Pony*, the last section in *The Long Valley*, is Jody's change from a childish, self-centered boy to a more mature young man capable of empathy. Jay Parini, poet, critic, and novelist, was a research fellow at Christ Church College, Oxford, England. He is the author of three collections of poetry and four novels.

The Long Valley had appeared when Steinbeck was just past the midpoint in writing *The Grapes of Wrath*. And while it did not sell quite on the same large scale as *Tortilla Flat* or *Of Mice and Men*, it made it onto the bestseller lists: an unusual thing, then and now, for a volume of stories. His movie agent, Annie Laurie Williams, wrote to Steinbeck on September 23: "*The Long Valley* is getting marvelous press." Indeed, it was. Stanley Young, in the *New York Times Book Review* (September 25, 1938), predicted that Steinbeck would "become a genuinely great American writer." The next day, in the *New Yorker*, Clifton Fadiman called the book "a remarkable collection by a writer who has so far neither repeated himself nor allowed himself a single careless sentence.". . .

The volume concludes with *The Red Pony*, a sequence of linked stories beloved by younger readers. (The final story in *The Long Valley* is called "The Leader of the People," and it became Part IV of *The Red Pony* when the tale was republished separately in book form by Viking in 1945.) *The Red Pony* is really a brief, episodic novel in which Steinbeck traces the emotional development of a boy, Jody Tiflin, from the narrow self-concern typical of children to a more compassionate view of the world. In keeping with this development, the first story, "The Gift," turns on the gift of a red

Excerpted from Jay Parini, *John Steinbeck: A Biography* (New York: Henry Holt, 1995). Reprinted with permission.

pony, which signals Jody's movement toward responsibility. He is, however, totally dependent on his father, whom he obeys "in everything without questions of any kind." Trust is the central issue in this story, and Jody trusts Billy Buck, a laconic farmhand, as well as his father. Billy promises to put the red pony in the barn if it rains, but he doesn't; the pony then catches cold, and it eventually dies, running off into the field to collapse. Buzzards swarm over the carcass, and Jody, hysterical, manages to catch and kill one of them, staring at the bird with an "impersonal and unafraid and detached" glare. The important but sad lesson Jody has learned is the fact of human fallibility, and his innocence is destroyed forever.

In "The Great Mountains," the second story, Steinbeck meditates on old age and its indignities. There is an old man on the Tiflin ranch whom Jody's father compares to a horse "who ought to be shot." But Jody, in whom compassion has been kindled by experience and contact with wise elders, strikes up a friendship with the old fellow, who radiates "a nameless sorrow" that is piteously evinced. In the end, the old man goes off, like the red pony, to die by himself in the mountains. Jody's perspective has been widened once again. Old age, like youth, has its tragic aspect.

The third story, "The Promise," concerns a young colt that Jody's father has promised the boy as a replacement for the red pony. Jody's responsibilities here are specific: His father insists that he take one of the mares to be mated; he must pay the stud fee with money he has earned himself. Further, he is to tend the mare for nearly a year, during the pregnancy—an unbearably long period for a young boy, who feels "reduced to peonage for the whole late spring and summer" as he waits for the horse, Nellie, to deliver her colt. When the time finally arrives, Nellie runs into trouble and has to be sacrificed for the sake of the colt. Jody gets what he wants in the end, a colt, but it comes with a huge sacrifice and another crucial lesson: old age must give way to youth.

"THE LEADER OF THE PEOPLE"— A POOR FIT WITH THE OTHERS

"The Leader of the People" was added later as a conclusion, although it doesn't really fit very well here; it concerns a visit from Mrs. Tiflin's father, who originally led the family from the East to the West Coast. The old man loves to recall his pioneering days, but as Jody's father complains, "He just goes on and on." Mrs. Tiflin tries patiently to explain her father's obsession to her impatient husband: "He led a wagon train clear across the plains to the coast, and when it was finished, his life was done." The problem was, the great trek came to an end, and the old man has since lost his function, which had a reality only in relation to the group. When the old man overhears his son-in-law complaining about him, he is struck by the truth of what he hears. "The crossing is finished," he says. "Maybe it should be forgotten, now it's done." He sits on the porch alone, depressed, contemplating his uselessness. Quite naturally, his grandson feels terribly sorry for him and brings a glass of lemonade in a gesture of empathy. In the discharge of this empathy Jody moves beyond the self-concern that was apparent in "The Promise." He has, in effect, reached another level of maturation.

The Red Pony is wonderfully simple in its affect, and the reader is only occasionally conscious of a "moral" lurking behind the tale. The California landscape glistens in the background, giving the narrative its texture and depth of field. While many of the adults in the stories are stereotypical, Jody Tiflin's gradual maturation is traced with affection, reserve, clarity, and compassion.

Steinbeck paid only slight attention to the reviews and sales of *The Long Valley*, and he seems not to have taken himself terribly seriously as a writer of stories in his later years. The argument has been made, however, that Steinbeck's short stories are actually superior to his novels [according to the critical summary made by Mary Rohrberger]. Even [French novelist] André Gide once said that Steinbeck wrote "nothing more perfect, more accomplished, than certain of his short stories." This is, however, a misguided attempt to overvalue one aspect of the writer's work at the expense of another. Steinbeck was certainly a capable and occasionally brilliant writer of short fiction, but the bulk of his novels overrides the fine impression made by a handful of stories. After the publication of *The Long Valley* he rarely attempted to write stories, sensing that the constraints of short fiction did not play to his strengths as a writer. He preferred the rhetorical sweep of long fiction, and to develop a character, he needed the space that is available in a novel.

CHAPTER 4

The Red Pony on Film

READINGS ON
THE RED PONY

The Red Pony
Adapted for Film

Joseph R. Millichap

Joseph R. Millichap contrasts the written version of
The Red Pony with the film version. After explaining
Steinbeck's story sequence, Millichap recounts the
scenes in the film from opening to closing shot, explaining camera angles, commenting on the effectiveness of scenes, and evaluating the actors' roles. Joseph
R. Millichap taught English at the University of Mon-
tana, Missoula, and Western Kentucky University,
Bowling Green. He is the author of the novel *People of
the Pilgrim Hawk* and many television scripts.

The Red Pony was a labor of love both for the writer and
Lewis Milestone, who in 1939 had directed the sensitive
screen version of *Of Mice and Men*. Having become friendly
during the production of the earlier film, the pair had discussed the possibility of bringing *The Red Pony* to the screen
as early as 1940. However, various other projects kept both
men from working on the scheme until 1947 when they went
into partnership to make the film version. A number of
problems delayed both the production and its release until
1949. Steinbeck served as screenwriter, his only solo adaptation of one of his own works, while Milestone took on the
jobs of both producer and director.

Unfortunately, though aided by a capable production
team and cast, Steinbeck and Milestone turned out only a
competent screen version which proved a moderate success,
both critically and financially. The artistic climate of the
Hollywood studio system prevented a fully realized film version of *The Red Pony*. *Of Mice and Men*, though an artistic
success, did not fit box-office formula and so had failed
commercially even when in desperation the Roach studios
had tried to peddle it as a sex shocker. If similar financial

failure were to be avoided, *The Red Pony* had to be refashioned and pigeonholed as a kind of kiddy Western about a boy and his horse. The film's conclusion, altered to a stock happy ending, is representative of the general transformation of plot, character, and theme in this cinematic adaptation of one of Steinbeck's finest works of fiction.

Steinbeck evidently began *The Red Pony* fairly early in his career; his letters indicate he was working on a "pony story" in 1933, and the first two sections of the story sequence, "The Gift" and "The Great Mountains" were published in the *North American Review* for November and December of that year. The third section, "The Promise" did not appear in *Harper's* until 1937, and "The Leader of the People," the final section, was not added until the publication of *The Long Valley* in 1938. However, manuscript and textual evidence indicates that the later sections were written some time before their publication, not very long after the first two stories. The four sections are connected by common characters, settings, and themes, forming a clearly unified story sequence which was published separately as *The Red Pony* in 1945.

THE STORY SEQUENCE IN THE BOOK

All four stories involve the maturation of Jody Tiflin, a boy of about ten when the action opens. The time is about 1910 and the setting is the Tiflin ranch in the Salinas Valley, where Jody lives with his father, Carl, his mother, Ruth, and the hired hand, a middle-aged cowboy named Billy Buck. From time to time they are visited by Jody's grandfather, a venerable old man who led one of the first wagon trains to California. "The Gift," the first story in the sequence, concerns Jody's red pony, which he names Gabilan, after the nearby mountain range. The pony soon becomes a symbol of the boy's growing maturity and his developing knowledge of the natural world. Later he carelessly leaves the pony out in the rain, and it takes cold and dies, despite Billy Buck's efforts to save it. Thus Jody learns of nature's cruel indifference to human wishes. In the second section, "The Great Mountains," the Tiflin ranch is visited by a former resident, Gitano, an aged Chicano laborer raised in the now vanished *hacienda.*[1] Old Gitano had come home to die. In a debate

1. Spanish for farm

which recalls [American poet] Robert Frost's poem "The Death of the Hired Man," Carl persuades Ruth that they cannot take Old Gitano in, but as in the poem their dialogue proves pointless. Stealing a broken-down nag significantly named Easter, the old man rides off into the mountains to die in dignity. Again, Jody has discovered some of the complex, harsh reality of adult life.

In "The Promise," the third story, Jody learns of the inextricable connections between life and death, when to get the boy another colt, his father has one of the mares put to stud. However, the birth is complicated, and Billy Buck must kill the mare to save the colt. "The Leader of the People," brings the sequence to an end with another vision of death and change. Jody's grandfather comes to visit, retelling his time-worn stories of the great wagon crossing. Carl Tiflin cruelly hurts the old man by revealing that nobody but Jody is really interested in these repetitious tales. The grandfather realizes that Carl is right, but later he tells Jody that the adventurous stories weren't the point, but that his message was "Westering" itself. For the grandfather, "Westering" was a force like [historian Frederick Jackson] Turner's frontier, the source of American identity; now with the close of the frontier, "Westering" has ended. Westerners had degenerated to petty landholders like Carl Tiflin and aging cowboys like Billy Buck. In his grandfather's ramblings, Jody discovers a sense of mature purpose, and by the conclusion of the sequence he too can hope to be a leader of the people.

This story sequence is among Steinbeck's finest work. *The Red Pony* traces Jody's initiation into adult life with both realism and sensitivity, a balance which Steinbeck did not always achieve. The vision of the characters caught up in the harsh world of nature is balanced by their deep human concerns and commitments. The evocation of the ranch setting in its vital beauty is matched only in the author's finest works, such as *Of Mice and Men.* Steinbeck's symbols grow naturally out of this setting, and nothing in the story sequence seems forced into a symbolic pattern, as is true in the later works. In its depiction of an American variation of a universal experience, *The Red Pony* deserves comparison with the finest of American fiction, especially initiation tales such as [William] Faulkner's *The Bear* or [Ernest] Hemingway's Nick Adams stories.

ADAPTATIONS, ACTORS, AND PRODUCTION

Obviously, such a fine work of fiction had much to offer as a film, but it also represented some inherent difficulties. Steinbeck's story sequence is episodic, unified only by continuities of character, setting, and theme. These subtle variations on the theme of intiation had to be woven together and considerably cut for a screenplay. The exigencies of production forced Steinbeck to eliminate completely one of the four stories in the sequence, "The Great Mountains," and to severely cut another one, "The Promise." For adaptation purposes the remaining stories were then spliced to form a sequential narrative of considerably less complexity. In addition Steinbeck concluded his screenplay with a Hollywood happy ending that completely distorts the meaning of his original work.

Though characters, particularly Jody and his grandfather, are types, they are complex ones and therefore hard to realize. Of the cast only Robert Mitchum as the ranchhand Billy Buck remains convincing throughout the movie, and even Mitchum is too youthful and idealized. In many ways he seems a variation of another idealized screen character created by [actor] Alan Ladd a few years later in *Shane* (1953). As in George Stevens's film, though not in Steinbeck's story, the relationship between the ranch wife and the hired hand becomes a complicating issue in Milestone's movie. Myrna Loy and Mitchum, who were given the star billing for the film, create a sense of romance between the characters they portray. Perhaps trying to escape her role as William Powell's sophisticated spouse in the Thin Man series, Miss Loy strains to be sweet in her role as Alice Tiflin. (For some reason, Steinbeck changed the name of all three Tiflins from novel to screenplay.) Fred Tiflin is weaker and less interesting than in the story sequence, and he is made even less so by Shepperd Strudwick's hangdog interpretation. Louis Calhern is adequate though uninspired as the grandfather. However the major casting problem is with the protagonist, Tom Tiflin, as portrayed by Peter Miles. Perhaps no child star could capture the complexity of this role, as it is much easier to write about sensitive children than to film them. Young Miles's portrayal often seems rather sugared and his anger at the world more or less a tantrum. The only other characters of note are a group of Tom's schoolmates, whose Our Gang antics make Peter Miles's performance seem peerless by comparison.

The other production values are good. The film was shot on location at a Salinas Valley ranch that looks very much like the one used in *Of Mice and Men*. As in the earlier film, settings are very well handled with realistic interiors and natural exteriors. Tony Gaudio's color cinematography makes use of natural, muted tones which often suggest the best of regional American painting and sometimes Wesley Dennis's illustrations for the 1945 edition of *The Red Pony*. Perhaps the best single feature of the film is the powerful score by Aaron Copeland, who had also scored *Of Mice and Men*; both scores later became concert favorites. As in his earlier work for Milestone, Copeland matches the mood of the visuals.

THE FILM'S STRONG OPENING

Milestone opens the film with a pre-title sequence which clearly recalls *Of Mice and Men* in both visual and musical imagery. As in the earlier film, the sequence establishes a complex relationship between the human characters and the natural world. First the camera pans over a scenic spot of the dark mountains, at last establishing the ranch house and outbuildings nestled in a hollow. A narrative voice-over establishes time and place:

> In central California many small ranches sit in the hollows of the skirts of the Coast Range Mountains. Some, the remnants of old and gradually disintegrating homesteads; some the remains of Spanish grants. To one of them in the foothills to the west of Salinas Valley, the dawn comes, as it comes to a thousand others.

The natural cycle of day begins earlier for the animal than the human world. In quick sequence Milestone close-ups a crowing rooster on a post, a gobbling turkey in a tree, two dogs shaking slowly from sleep, a softly hooting owl in another tree, and finally a rabbit. The dogs and the owl respond to the presence of the rabbit just beyond camera range; then the owl swoops for a kill. The natural world presents a complex beauty, marked by rhythms of life and death, of beginnings and endings, of ever repeated cycles. This sequence ends when Billy Buck walks out of the bunkhouse and into the barn, lighting a lantern to check the horses. The light falls on the cover of the novel, which in turn opens to present the production data—a common title device in the 1940s. All in all like many Milestone films, *The*

Red Pony opens quite well, but, unfortunately, it does not sustain the artistic intensity of the beginning.

After the titles fade, Billy whistles and calls his mare, Rosie; then Billy fondles her and begins a morning ritual of feeding and currying. Milestone cuts to the farmhouse where Alice Tiflin is preparing breakfast; she stops and walks out on the porch to ring the triangle that calls the rest of the characters. Two quick close-ups show the awakening Fred Tiflin and his son, Tommy. Billy arrives at the kitchen first, but he waits for the others to enter before him, subtly establishing the relationship of the owner and hired hand, as well as the equation of Tommy and Fred as the immature members of the family and of Alice and Billy as those who accept adult responsibility.

Inside the kitchen some homey bits are done: close-ups of cooking ham and eggs, the boy washing behind the ears, and the father kidding Billy about a trip into town. At this point the screenplay includes a long conversation—not included in the final print—about Billy's mare, Rosie, who is expecting a colt in a few months. Probably Milestone felt the discussion slowed the development of the story, even though it foreshadowed the symbolic birth of Rosie's colt at the conclusion. However, the film does add scenes to the story at this point. After Billy and Tom leave, Alice and Fred Tiflin's exchange about Tom's attachment for the ranch hand clearly indicates the father's sense of inadequacy and his jealousy of his hired hand. The reason for his anxiety is revealed in the next sequence, in which Tom asks Billy to show him the newspaper clipping reporting Rosie's victory in the Sacramento Stock Show. As the best hand with horses in the area, Billy is nature's nobleman for young Tom, an extension of his grandfather's days of glory in the Old West.

SCENES TO ENGAGE THE AUDIENCE'S EMOTIONS AND CURIOSITY

Milestone dramatizes these feelings, as Tom sets off for school, fantasizing that he and Billy are knights leading a troop of splendid soldiers. This interpolated sequence includes an animated background which seems right out of a Walt Disney production. Of course, it is intended to visualize the boy's fantasy life, but it only establishes a kids' picture undertone which would have been best avoided here. This mood is underlined by the next scene when Tom's reverie is

disturbed by the other school children. In his story, Steinbeck handles both of these sequences in a single sentence:
"At the crossroads over the bridge he met two friends and the
three of them walked to school together, making ridiculous
strides and being rather silly." When this sentence is trans-
lated into a combination of Disney and Our Gang, the film
quickly loses much of the power promised by the literary
source and anticipated in the strong opening sequence.

Meanwhile, back at the ranch, Alice and Fred talk about
the expected arrival of the grandfather, and we are introduced to themes from "The Leader of the People." In the film
the grandfather owns the ranch and lives with the Tiflin
family, and this establishes a relationship which is very different from the one in the story. Fred is made a childish dependent, much like his son, Tom. In this conversation it becomes apparent that he doesn't much like the ranch and
longs to return to town life in San Jose. Alice is more thoroughly identified with her father as a symbol of a natural
tradition also represented by Billy Buck. When Tom returns
from school in the next sequence Alice remembers Fred's
complaint that the boy neglects his school work to knock
about with Billy. She even repeats her husband's very words.
"There are other things to know besides ranching." Her
heart is not in her scolding, and she soon allows Tom to
leave his books and go off to prowl the ranch yard. Here he
feeds the chickens and performs other chores in Tom
Sawyer or Huck Finn fashion while Milestone makes a nice
overhead shot of the boy circled by the clucking hens. However, animation changes the fowl to white circus horses
prancing around a ring while Tom directs them with a long
ringmaster's whip. The screenplay indicates that both of
these animated fantasy sequences were to have been longer,
but Milestone wisely cut them down; he would have been
even wiser to cut them out completely.

"THE GIFT" BLENDED WITH "THE LEADER OF THE PEOPLE"

This time Tom is pulled from his reverie by the call of his ar-
riving grandfather. This scene and the dinner that follows
are taken almost verbatim from "The Leader of the People"
and intertwined with the themes of "The Gift." Although this
process creates some dislocations, it does make the grandfather's story seem less of a digression from the process of
Tom's maturation. When Tom tells the grandfather that he

plans a mouse hunt after the haystacks are leveled, the grandfather compares the hunt to the cavalry's slaughter of the Indians on the frontier, and Tom learns that the Western experience was not all the imaginings of dime novels. His initiation into the complex realities of adult life continues at dinner when his father slights his grandfather at every opportunity, clearly demonstrating the immaturity hinted at in earlier scenes.

After dinner, the red pony is presented. Billy and Fred bought the animal in town, where it was left stranded by the collapse of a traveling show. Tom, of course, is ecstatic, both with his pony and its show saddle. He promises to take the best possible care of the animal, and to perform all of his other chores faithfully in repayment for the gift. Fred soon leaves, with a final threat to sell the pony if he ever finds it hungry or dirty, and Billy Buck takes over as the father surrogate, promising to help Tom raise the best horse in the region. The pony will be trained well enough to ride by Thanksgiving, Billy assures the boy. Clearly, Gabilan, the red pony, represents a link with primal nature within the natural process of a boy's maturation.

Meanwhile, the child in Tom is revealed when the next day he brings his school friends home to see the pony. Once again the film falls to the level of *My Friend Flicka* (1943), as the kids cut some cute capers only briefly mentioned in Steinbeck's original work. Better scenes are created when Milestone shows Billy and Tom working with the animal. In many of these ranch scenes the director achieves the naturalistic poetry he created from California ranch life in *Of Mice and Men*. When Tom trains the horse with a rope and halter, the camera pans for 180 degrees on the resulting circle of movement and then rises for a down shot, a composition which clearly reduplicates Wesley Dennis's frontispiece for the illustrated edition of the stories.

The following two sequences combine the climactic action of both "The Leader of the People" and "The Gift." At breakfast, after Tom has shown how well he has trained his horse, his father reacts by bullying both the boy and the grandfather. Thinking that the old man is out of earshot Fred complains bitterly about the grandfather's garrulous tales of his days as wagonmaster. However, the old man overhears him from behind the doorway, and this knowledge embarrasses the whole group gathered for breakfast. Milestone handles this scene very nicely in terms of quick close-up re-action shots that capture its inherent drama. Fred apologizes and prepares to retreat to his parents' home in San Jose, a clear desertion of his responsibilities to his family and the ranch. The grandfather, who must reassess his relationships and his attitudes, concludes that he has indeed bored every-one with his tales. Yet he insists that his purpose was right, he wanted not to tell of wild adventures, but to capture the essence of the Westward movement in his talk. He muses:

> . . . We carried life our here and set it down and planted it the way ants carry eggs and I was the leader. The westerin' was big as God and the slow steps that made up the movement piled up . . . and piled up until the continent was crossed. . . . Then we come down to the sea and it was done. . . . Well, that's what I oughtta be tellin' instead a' the stories. The Sto-ries ain't what I want to say.

Tom intuitively understands what his grandfather means, and his sympathy for the old man is another indication of his developing maturity. Yet he is not ready to be a leader of the people himself. The experience of loss and death await him.

THE PONY'S SICKNESS AND DEATH

Partially because of his own carelessness, partially because of Billy Buck's, his beloved pony is left in the corral through a cold and rainy afternoon. When Tom returns from school—a Disney-like scene with byplay between the kids and the teacher played by Margaret Hamilton, the Wicked Witch of the West from *The Wizard of Oz* (1939)—the pony is shivering and sneezing. Tom guiltily accuses Billy Buck of having failed in his responsibility. "You said it wouldn't rain," he whines in protest. The boy has learned another lesson: the adults in his world are fallible. As the pony sickens, he learns more of nature's indif-ference to human wishes. He may fantasize all he wants about his "trick pony," but nature plays the final trick. Billy cannot save the weakening animal in spite of a promise to pull the pony through. Finally Billy opens a hole in the animal's wind-pipe in a futile, last attempt to save its life. In a discreet reaction shot, Milestone captures the boy's sensitive response to blood and pain. Naturally, this scene is more powerfully depicted in the story than in a film which had to avoid shocking the sensi-bilities of its intended juvenile audience. Even so, some con-temporary reviews complained that both this scene and that of the pony's death were too harsh for children.

A couple of sentimental scenes intrude before the pony's death and Tom's fight with buzzards. The mother recalls the father from San Jose, and he pledges his love for her, the boy, and the ranch. On Thanksgiving, when Tom's friends come expecting to see him and ride the pony for the first time, he is forced to put them off with a story about the pony being shod in town. His pride won't allow him to share the hurt he feels for his dying pony. Later that same evening, Tom beds down in the pony's stall, but the animal wanders from the barn, seeking the hills to die in nature. Waking from his fitful sleep, the boy follows the pony's footprints up into the scrubby brush, and looking up, Tom and the camera see a circle of buzzards. Tom runs along the crest of a bare hill as the camera follows him in a long tracking shot. Then in a down angle it catches his running reflection in the pool of a stream; suddenly he stops and reverses direction. The camera looks at the dead pony through Tom's eyes. A buzzard has come down on the body, and as Tom watches another lands near the head. The boy races back down the bank, chasing the buzzards; then the camera follows him past the pony as he grabs a thrusting bird. The camera cuts quickly between the boy and the buzzard, as the frantic bird pecks at him wildly. The bird's beak and claws cut Tom in several places, and as blood soaks his ripped shirt he finds a sharp stone and smashes the buzzard with it. Billy and Fred come running in just as the boy strangles the bird in one final burst of rage. In a line of dialogue taken from the story, Fred tells Tom that the buzzard hasn't killed his pony; and Billy, more perceptive in this crisis, snaps: "Of course he knows it. Use your head, man, can't you see how he'd feel about it?"

It is Billy, not Fred, who carries Tom back to the ranch house. As they retrace the muddy tracks left by the dying pony, Billy expiates his own guilt in the pony's death and the boy's disillusionment by promising to give him Rosie's colt when it is born. This development is taken from the third story in Steinbeck's sequence, "The Promise," in which the events take place about a year after the red pony's death. Here the action is shortened as Billy's mare is nearing the end of her gestation cycle. At first Tom refuses to take any interest in Billy's promise. He has been too badly hurt by the loss of the red pony to chance his feelings on another horse. Instead he rejects Billy, his family and his friends at school.

In one fine scene he sits reading and is shown reflected by the stream seen earlier in the death of the pony; Rosie coming to drink nuzzles him gently, but he rejects her as well.

THE NEW COLT AND A HAPPY ENDING

Yet as Spring opens out, the sense of life overpowers the memory of death. Tom again talks to his family and his friends; he begins to play with his dogs and Rosie; finally, he asks Billy for the colt. Billy promises that the mare will drop a fine colt with no complications. But again nature ignores human desires. In a scene recalling the earlier unsuccessful operation on the red pony, Billy encounters unexpected problems with the birth of Rosie's colt. Evidently, it is turned the wrong way in the mother's womb, and the horseman must choose between killing the mother or the colt. In the story the boy watches in horror as Billy brutally fulfills his promise by killing poor Rosie in the process of delivering a beautiful colt. The screenplay, probably under studio pressure, opts for an easier conclusion.

Billy makes the decision to kill Rosie, but Tom grabs the knife and runs off to the house. By the time the ranchhand has caught up with him, the rest of the family are able to prevail on Billy to spare the mother animal. The central group is seen through the doors of Tom's room, then of the house, then of the barn, as they race back to the birth scene. Suddenly, they all stop in amazement as the camera pans them in a row along the side of the stall. Next a point-of-view shot reveals the surprise; somehow in the few moments she was left alone, Rosie has discreetly brought a perfect colt into the world. The pan of the characters is repeated as they all laugh in happy reaction to the bounty of nature. The film's final shots are of Tom riding the mature colt—which bears a decided resemblance to the original red pony—across the beautiful foothills of the Gabilan Mountains.

Of course, this conclusion alters the theme of Steinbeck's story sequence. The author himself included it in his screenplay, perhaps because he felt this final comprise was justified by the realistic presentation of the earlier death of the red pony. Yet this last alteration only typifies the general changes in mood which studio production wrought in the film version of the story sequence. Steinbeck's naturalistic yet beautiful Salinas Valley is transformed into the pastoral dreamland of *National Velvet* (1944) or *The Yearling* (1947), or *So Dear to My Heart* (1949). Some of the characters, particularly Mitchum's Billy Buck, some of the scenes, particularly the death of the red pony, some of the settings, particularly the barn, and some of the themes are still reminiscent of Steinbeck's. In its best places the film adds Milestone's graceful visual touch and Copeland's powerful musical score to the author's naturalistic, yet lyrical, vision.

Although Milestone's *The Red Pony* is not as fully realized as Steinbeck's original story sequence, it remains a reasonable film adaptation, one much better than most in its generic pattern. Nevertheless, Steinbeck's complicity in its artistic compromise indicates how much his ideals had been altered by Hollywood. There were no telegrams to protest the alteration of his work or asking to remove his name. Perhaps he needed the money because of his divorce; perhaps he wanted to see his name on the silver screen once more. In any case, Steinbeck and Milestone had both declined as artists since their happier collaboration on *Of Mice and Men* in 1939.

The Red Pony as Story Cycle and Film

Warren French

Warren French gives a thorough account of how *The Red Pony* evolved into a film. He first analyzes the four sections as a story cycle and as archetypal forms; he then explains the structure and content of the film. Warren French, scholar, critic, and editor, is the author of *John Steinbeck, Frank Norris, A Companion to "The Grapes of Wrath," The South in Film,* and *J.D. Salinger Revisited.*

The two works entitled *The Red Pony* are of unique interest among John Steinbeck's fictions as the only example of the writer's being solely responsible for the film script version of one of his earlier fictional works. The pair is, in fact, of uncommon interest in American literature and twentieth-century writing generally because few major artists have produced such a pair of related works. I do not speak here of Steinbeck's adapting his earlier work for another medium, because that term does not adequately describe this particular transformation.

The original *Red Pony* is a compilation of four short stories that were first published independently and that are among Steinbeck's earliest preserved writings. "The Gift," which is the only one of the four stories about the red circus pony that provides the title for the cycle, appeared in the *North American Review* (November 1933) and was followed the next month by "The Great Mountains," narrating another experience of Jody Tiflin, the boy who had owned the pony, in the same literary journal.

Although the third story in the cycle, "The Promise," appears to have been written at the same time as the other two stories, in the early 1930s, it did not appear in *Harper's* monthly magazine until October 1937; and the final story,

Excerpted from Warren French, "*The Red Pony* as Story Cycle and Film," in *The Short Novels of John Steinbeck: Critical Essays with a Checklist to Steinbeck Criticism*, edited by Jackson J. Benson (Durham, NC: Duke University Press, 1990). Copyright © 1990. All rights reserved. Reprinted with permission.

"The Leader of the People," was not published in the United States until Steinbeck collected his early short stories in *The Long Valley* in 1938, although the manuscript was in a book with other stories that had been published as early as 1934, and the story had appeared in the English magazine *Argosy* in August 1936. In *The Long Valley* only the first three stories mentioned above appeared under the collective title "The Red Pony." All four stories were not collected under this title until the first separate publication of *The Red Pony* in a large-format edition lyrically illustrated by Wesley Dennis in 1945.

Even though the four stories were not brought together in this final form until more than a decade after their composition, they are closely linked accounts of Jody Tiflin's significant formative experiences during the crucial period of his painful passage from childhood into adolescence. "The Promise" continues the story of "The Gift." The other two stories are not so specifically linked to that pair or each other, but they all deal with similar kinds of experiences of continuing characters, which makes the quartet what [critic] Forrest L. Ingram calls a short story cycle, "a set of stories so linked to one another that the reader's experience of each one is modified by his experience of the others." Longer collections exemplifying this genre are James Joyce's *Dubliners* and Dylan Thomas's *Portrait of the Artist as a Young Dog*, and, among American writings, William Faulkner's *The Unvanquished*, Sherwood Anderson's *Winesburg, Ohio*, and Steinbeck's *The Pastures of Heaven* and *Tortilla Flat*.

THE STORY CYCLE

In "The Gift" Jody Tiflin is given his first horse (an act symbolizing the ranch boy's initiation into manhood), a red pony that his father has bought from a bankrupt traveling circus, where it had been trained to perform tricks. Jody begins to develop a sense of responsibility for more than routine chores when he is charged with caring for the pony and training it. When the delicate show animal is left exposed to the elements by Billy Buck, the ranch hand whom Jody childishly trusts, it becomes ill and dies. The boy expresses his frustration by killing a carrion buzzard that tries to feed on the carcass.

The only connection between "The Gift" and "The Great Mountains," the story that always appears second in collections, is the character of Jody. The time of the action in this story in relation to any others in the cycle is not specified, but it is usually taken for granted that it occurs some time after the autumn death of the red pony and before the birth of the colt that replaces it in "The Gift." This somber story tells of Jody's encounter with Gitano, an aged Mexican-American whose family once owned the land that is now the Tiflin family ranch. Gitano has come home to die, but Jody's father will not allow the old man to stay on the property. Jody watches helplessly as Gitano disappears with a dying horse named Easter into the great dark mountains that brood over the valley.

The third story, "The Promise," picks up where "The Gift" leaves off, with the ranch hand Billy Buck, who feels responsible for the death of the red pony, promising Jody the next colt of one of the ranch's mares, Nellie, if Jody will take her to the stud and care for her during the long pregnancy. Jody carries out these duties faithfully; but, unfortunately, Billy Buck's promise can be fulfilled only by sacrificing the life of the mare when the unborn colt moves into a position that makes its live delivery otherwise impossible.

The relationship of the time of the action of the last story, "The Leader of the People," to the others is not clear, although since it takes place in March, when Jody apparently does not have a horse, it seems most likely that it occurs just before the spring climax of "The Promise," which narrates the events of an entire year. In contrast, the final story relates the events of only a single twenty-four-hour period during which Jody's visiting maternal grandfather, who has guided parties of pioneers on their dangerous migrations to the West Coast, makes the disheartening discovery that his time, like old Gitano's in "The Great Mountains," is over and that the next generation is annoyed by his constant retelling of the story of his vital role in the conquest of the West. Jody, however, is entranced by his grandfather's stories, to the annoyance of his sedentary father. When Jody expresses the hope that he may some day lead the people himself, his grandfather gloomily observes that there is no place left to go and that the spirit of "westering" has died out.

Like most of Steinbeck's early fictions, these four stories have strong dramatic structures that would make it possible for them to be adapted with little change as successive episodes in a motion picture depicting the crucial events in a perceptive and impressionable child's maturing into a responsible young man. Although specific links are not provided between all four stories, they are not simply autonomous tales of Jody's separate confrontations with a series of crises that provide his rites of passage into manhood. As I pointed out in summarizing the interrelationships of the stories in an analysis of their individual and collective meanings in my book *John Steinbeck*, the cycle depicts the way in which this boy has learned compassion in the course of undergoing four crucial tests very much like those imposed upon appellants for knighthood in the Middle Ages, a subject that fascinated Steinbeck.

These experiences teach Jody "the fallibility of man," through a trusted mentor's inadvertent neglect of the delicate red pony; "the wearing out of man," through old Gitano's death; "the unreliability of nature," through the death of the mare Nellie as the result of a defect in a natural process that man is powerless to remedy; and "the exhaustion of nature" that left Jody's grandfather and other leaders of the westward migration of his generation sitting along the Pacific shore hating the ocean because it has left them with no more lands for their restless "westering" spirits to conquer.

THE FILM COULD HAVE RETAINED THE STORY CYCLE

This same progressive maturation of the boy's sensibilities could have been presented through a four-part film following faithfully the original stories. A precedent existed for such films in the work of French director Julien Duvivier, who, while working in exile in the United States during World War II, had experimented in *Tales of Manhattan* and *Flesh and Fantasy* with fashioning feature-length films from separate but related episodes (the former consisted of three short fables about different wearers of the same full-dress suit). While these frivolous efforts to divert and lift the spirits of war-weary moviegoers lacked the high seriousness of Steinbeck's stories, they demonstrated how visual motifs as well as verbal devices could be used to link episodes that could also be viewed as autonomous presentations.

However, nothing of the structure of the original story cycle is retained in Steinbeck's film script. The closely connected stories of "The Gift" and "The Promise" are used, with some important changes, to provide a single, continuous plot line for the eighty-six-minute film, so that it is much more like a conventional film derived from a traditional novel than it is an attempt to duplicate the form of the story cycle. Although Steinbeck derives most of the material for the film from the stories, he drops a good deal, including the entire second story, "The Great Mountains." He also adds some entirely new material and makes a drastic and controversial change in the climax of the film to provide an entirely new upbeat ending.

If a producer who had acquired the rights to an original work made such extensive changes in it, admirers of the original could justifiably raise cries of protest against the treatment of the source. With *The Red Pony*, however, these drastic alterations were made not just with the author's consent but by the author himself as part of a project in which he collaborated and over which he exercised artistic control. Steinbeck was obviously not interested in simply transferring his story cycle to the screen; he wished to tell the story of Jody Tiflin's initiation into manhood in a way that he deemed suited to the new medium.

THE STORY CYCLE EXEMPLIFIES ARCHETYPAL FORMS

Before we examine the film version of *The Red Pony*, however, something more needs to be said about the complex nature of the original story cycle. In an article assessing the significance of Steinbeck's contribution to American literature, I moved beyond my original thesis about the story cycle's portraying a particular young man's coming of age in a particular culture to argue that the four stories viewed collectively also provide a dramatization of [critic] Northrop Frye's famous schematic analysis in "The Archetypes of Literature" (1951) of the archetypal forms of literary genres as they constituted a seasonal cycle of the year from birth to death and rebirth.[1]

In that article I observed that Steinbeck does not begin his cycle, as might be anticipated, with a story of spring and rebirth, but with a tale of what Frye describes as "the sunset, autumn and death phase" that provides the archetypes of "tragedy and elegy," myths of "the dying god, of violent death and sacrifice, and of the isolation of the hero," terms that are all precisely applicable to the ironically titled tale of "The Gift."

---

1. In his unpublished "Narration," Steinbeck stated that he was aware of the mythic implications of his tales. Frye may have used Steinbeck's work with traditional classics in formulating his theories.

The article then proceeds to describe the second story, "The Great Mountains," as a winter's tale, even though it begins on a summer afternoon. The heat of the day, however, is in contrast to the coldness of the situation, and the ironically sunny backdrop renders particularly pathetic the tale as an example of what Frye describes as "myths of darkness and dissolution," "of floods and the return of chaos, of the defeat of the hero, and Götterdämmerung myths," as an old man returns to his birthplace to die only to be denied this attempt to recover his history.

"The Promise," however, is a spring tale of dawn and birth, especially if one sees the real focus of the tale as the colt that is ripped from its dying mother's womb, like heroes of ancient legend. This extraction of life from death provides a pattern of seasonal rebirth, of the revival and resurrection that Frye calls the archetype of romance.

The most ironic of the four tales, in the way in which it follows a mythical pattern and yet subverts it, is "The Leader of the People." Jody's grandfather's reminiscences of "westering" do contain an archetypal summer myth of "apotheosis, of the sacred marriage, and of entering into paradise"; but the entry into paradise it describes—the marriage of wild nature and civilization—is now in the past, and the paradise has been lost. "Westering" has died out among the people, and the mouse hunt that Jody suggests to his grandfather as an alternative in the boy's aspiration to become a new leader himself shows Steinbeck, like [American poet] Robert Frost in "The Oven Bird," depicting his contemporaries trying to determine "what to make of a diminished thing."

The point of comparing Steinbeck's stories with Northrop Frye's theories promulgated a quarter century later is to suggest that Steinbeck created not just a story of one youth's coming of age but a movingly realistic tale that recapitulates a basic pattern in human experience, as he acknowledged when he wrote in the proposed introduction to [American composer] Aaron Copland's *The Red Pony* suite, derived from the composer's score for the film, "the path has been travelled before [and] the little boy is not a fresh created uniqueness in the universe."

THE STRUCTURE AND CONTENT OF THE FILM

The modest motion picture, however, fails to live up to a mythic model as successfully as the original story cycle, for some of the tough truths that Steinbeck faced unflinchingly in raising his childhood memories to mythical proportions are omitted (like the death of old Gitano) or mitigated (like the death of the mare Rosie) in the film. It needs, therefore, to be approached on its own terms as an autonomous work of art rather than denigrated for failing to do justice to the potential of the story cycle.

The question of what the film retains of the story cycle can be dealt with briefly. The carefully structured film may be divided into twenty-four episodes, or "sequences," as groups of related scenes are usually called in film analysis. (A "scene" is a single continuous action, though it may be composed of a variety of "shots"—each the product of a single, uninterrupted running of a camera—taken from different perspectives.) It is on the basis of these sequences that the relationship of the material in the film to the stories can be most precisely calculated.

Actually, most of the original material reused for the film comes from the opening story, "The Gift." More than half of the film's twenty-four sequences (thirteen) and more than half of the film's length (about forty-five of its eighty-six minutes) employ material from this original story of the red pony. The pony's death, which occurs at the end of the first story in the cycle, occurs near the end of the film. Only the last twelve minutes are used to relate the events of the year that passes during the narration of "The Promise," the third story in the cycle. Nothing is used in the film from the second story, "The Great Mountains"; and the grandfather's confrontation with Jody's father that provides the climax for the story is interpolated into the action from "The Gift" early in the film.

On the other hand, about four minutes of new material that could have provided the basis for a previously untold story about Jody's father taking a trip to town, during which he is tempted to give up the ranch and move the family back to where he could work in the family store, is introduced early in the film. While this could also be shaped into a winter's tale about the death of a dream and a loss of the land, this middle-class dilemma provides no match for the chilling dramatic power of the tale of the disinherited old man.

A major change is also made in the ending of "The Promise," which now provides the climax for the film. In the original story Billy Buck is obliged to kill the mare in order to deliver her colt and fulfill his promise to Jody. In the film, however, tragedy is averted so that a happy ending may be manufactured. Billy Buck only dreams that the colt has been mispositioned and that Rosie (as the mare is called in the film) must be killed. Although the next morning he makes preparations in expectation of the worst, Jody creates a distraction that allows Rosie to make a perfectly normal delivery unaided (and unseen, since the film was produced in the days when a strict production code forbade the showing of the birth of even animals on the screen). The film ends not with Jody being forced to recognize the frightful cost of his victory but with the whole family, including the grandfather (who in an unexplained change has apparently been reconciled to joining the son-in-law's household permanently), gathered in a circle beaming blissfully at the manger scene composed by the uninjured mare and her beautiful offspring.

THE FILM FOLLOWS HOLLYWOOD FORMULA

The title *The Red Pony* thus actually suits the film better than it does the cycle of four stories; but in its transformation it has become a simple variation on the typical Hollywood formula of the 1930s and 1940s—boy meets girl, boy loses girl, boy gets girl—though as is more fitting to a tale about a prepubescent ranch boy, the formula is altered to boy meets horse, boy loses horse, boy gets horse (not the same horse, it is true, but one better suited to the situation—a native of the region and not a pampered show pony—in a commonsensical amendment that [British novelist Charles] Dickens used to the basic formula in *David Copperfield*).

The four deaths (including the death of his grandfather's dream) that Jody must confront in the story cycle are thus reduced to one that is more than compensated for by the end of the film. Jody is able to maintain his place as a true son of the pioneers, having learned only that while those not suited to an environment, like his red pony, may be doomed, generally things work out for the best for good little boys who want to maintain Western traditions and not move to the city (as Rosasharn's despicable husband does in *The Grapes of Wrath*).

Despite Steinbeck's own statement in his proposed histrionic introduction to Aaron Copland's musical suite, that the character will never be a little boy again but has become a man, the cinematic Jody has not gone through the grueling initiation portrayed in the story cycle that might indeed prepare him for leadership of the people. Rather he has been given an assurance that if he is patient enough to learn from experience and control his temper, all will work out well in maintaining his established way of life.

EVALUATION OF THE FILM

Readers who come to the film from the story cycle may, of course, like [critic] Joseph Millichap, be upset to find that Jody at the end of the film has not become the man-boy who offers his dispirited grandfather the bitter refreshment of lemonade and a mouse hunt in a compassionate gesture, but rather one of what [American writer Ernest] Hemingway satirizes in "The Short Happy Life of Francis Macomber" as "the great American boy-men," who sometimes stay little boys all their lives.

Thus, although the film *The Red Pony* uses much of the same material as the story cycle, the differences from the earlier work far outnumber and outweigh the similarities. The most important difference is that the Jody in the film has not really begun to understand the meaning of his experiences, as is shown when he throws a tantrum like the earlier one during which he killed a buzzard just before the end of the film. Although the story cycle is frequently assigned to young readers to provide one of their earliest experiences with thoughtful literature, it is not likely that readers of Jody's own age can grasp the implications of the stories, which were written by an adult recalling boyhood experiences for readers of adult literary magazines.

The film of *The Red Pony* is, however, one of Hollywood's infrequent productions designed for a preteen audience, for which it provides a central figure with whom the audience can identify. This was evidently the audience that Steinbeck had in mind when he rearranged and altered his story line to reach the comfortable conclusion that things can work out all right as long as the family remains unified. No such reassurance is provided by the story cycle, which repeatedly portrays growing up as the terrifying process it always has been.

The story cycle is finally, in terms of Frye's archetypes, a comedy, but not a funny or even cheering one. It is an example of the classic mode of comedy—a myth about the ultimate triumph of common sense and goodwill over the delusions of what [British novelist] Jane Austen castigated as pride and prejudice, of sense over sensibility. *The Red Pony* story cycle foreshadowed what Steinbeck would achieve in his greatest works to follow—*Of Mice and Men, The Grapes of Wrath, Cannery Row,* even his harder-hitting film *The Forgotten Village. The Red Pony* as a film, however, is melodrama—a comforting work in which a situation that seems doomed to end in disaster is miraculously reversed at the last moment, if not by some *deus ex machina*[2], then by, as in this film, threatened calamity proving only a bad dream.

I am not, however, even in view of this comparative evaluation of these related but very different works, willing to go along with Joseph Millichap's disgruntled attribution of the changes for the worse that he perceives between the story cycle and the film to the notorious movie moguls who have often been justifiably impugned for even more dreadful transformations, like that of J.D. Salinger's short story "Uncle Wiggily in Connecticut" into the tear-jerking film *My Foolish Heart* that resulted in the author's refusal to sell film rights to any other works.

Millichap argues that Steinbeck's "complicity in the film's artistic compromises indicates how much his ideals had been altered by Hollywood" and goes on to complain that the author sent "no telegrams to protest the alteration of his work or asking to remove his name." He speculates that Steinbeck may have needed the money.

STEINBECK'S RELATED ACTIVITIES AND ISSUES

Beset by domestic problems as Steinbeck was in the late 1940s, he may indeed have needed money (though, for reasons to be explained subsequently, this film never made much money, and was, in fact, originally conceived by the novelist as a charitable contribution); but it would have been odd if he had complained about a script that he had written. With this film, unlike the dreadfully mutilated and financially disastrous *Tortilla Flat* and the subtly altered and triumphant *The Grapes of Wrath,* the author, and not the production company, was responsible for the changes; and he remained actively involved in the production. We need to look beyond Hollywood's usual whipping boys to find possi-

2. an unexpected, artificial, or improbable character, device, or event introduced suddenly in a work of fiction or drama to resolve a situation or untangle a plot

ble reasons for Steinbeck's drastic alterations of his basic story line two decades after he had shaped it and after his own life-style and point of view had been drastically changed by the harrowing experiences of becoming a celebrity, going through World War II and the breakup of two marriages, and becoming a father.

To begin with, by the time Steinbeck wrote the final script for the film, he knew a great deal about filmmaking, and his expectations about films were different from those that he had about his novels. He had become intensely interested in filmmaking back in the 1930s after viewing Pare Lorentz's much-admired documentaries *The Plow that Broke the Plains* and *The River*, sponsored by the federal government to help promote pioneering agricultural conservation projects for saving overexploited farmland. Steinbeck studied with Lorentz during the making of a medical documentary, *The Fight for Life*; and he went to Mexico to join another independent filmmaker, Herbert Kline, in producing the pseudo-documentary *The Forgotten Village* to escape the furor following the publication of *The Grapes of Wrath*. The hour-long film was released in 1940, about the time that Steinbeck first became involved in projects for filming *The Red Pony*.

The too-little-studied *Forgotten Village* is Steinbeck's closest work in plot and theme to *The Red Pony* story cycle. It tells the story of a remote village in the Mexican mountains that is stricken by a cholera plague from a polluted well and of the effort of public health authorities to break the grip of a *curandera* (woman witch doctor) on the superstitious indigenous community, whose language is not even Spanish but an ancient local tongue. The film appears to be a documentary because it was shot in a remote mountain village using a nonprofessional cast recruited locally; but like *The Red Pony* it is a fiction, telling through pictures and a voiced-over narration in English the idealistic story of a teenaged native boy's struggle to become a doctor who will be the savior of his community.

This Juan Diego very much resembles a slightly older Jody Tiflin in his irrepressible determination to become a leader of the people; the wrathful *curandera*, seeking to maintain her status and keep out the despised city doctors, resembles Jody's frustrated grandfather; the boy's family reflects the troubled irresolution of Jody's parents; and Billy

Buck is transformed into a determined and dedicated team of technicians from the public health service. The boy undergoes his rite of passage by defying his parents and disapproving community and making a frightening night journey to Mexico City to bring the light of modern medicine to the benighted community. Like the film version of *The Red Pony* (in contrast to the story cycle), *The Forgotten Village* is an upbeat work in which the boy succeeds in his quest. Actually it is even more upbeat than the later *Red Pony* because the incredibly resourceful Mexican lad does not even display Jody's residual childishness.

Subsequently Steinbeck took responsibility for two more film scripts. The script for *The Pearl* (1948) was written at the same time as the popular novelette and resembles it as closely as is possible in the different medium. *Viva Zapata!* (1952) grew out of Steinbeck's friendship with film director Elia Kazan and was conceived as the script for a film about the Mexican revolutionary leader Emiliano Zapata that Kazan filmed with Marlon Brando in the title role. Both films have distinctly upbeat endings. Despite the popularity of Steinbeck's novelette as wholesome moral fiction for high school students, the Mexican-made film version of *The Pearl* (there are slightly different versions with Spanish and English soundtracks) is rarely shown in the United States, because the realistic visualization of the fantastic tale makes the far-fetched nature of the story too conspicuous.

Although the incontrovertible facts of history forced Steinbeck and Kazan to kill off Zapata, they portray him as still present in spirit riding his white horse high on the mountains to lead his people to eventual liberty and light.

The implication of these comments is not that Steinbeck viewed the movies as a mass medium to be used only for dispensing upbeat inspirational messages, although the authorities governing the old Production Code certainly preferred that films be used that way. But that was the kind of message Steinbeck was disseminating through his works during the comparatively short period that he was involved in filmmaking. Though the much-debated final tableau in *The Grapes of Wrath* is only equivocally optimistic, his principal works of the 1940s and 1950s—*The Moon Is Down, The Wayward Bus, Cannery Row, Burning Bright, East of Eden*— end with hopeful, if not always convincing, visions in contrast to the bleakly ironic endings of the earlier *Cup of Gold,*

The Pastures of Heaven, Tortilla Flat, In Dubious Battle, and *Of Mice and Men.* Thus the ending of the film version of *The Red Pony* may not be in keeping with the ending of the story cycle, but it is certainly in keeping with the endings of the works that he was writing during the period when the film was produced.

A DECADE FROM IDEA TO FILM

The idea of basing a film upon the Jody Tiflin stories was a long time coming to fruition. As early as 1939 in a letter to his agent-confidante Elizabeth Otis, Steinbeck disclosed that [producer] Victor Fleming (at the peak of his fame for *Gone with the Wind*) and superstar Spencer Tracy, who had starred in the film adaptation of Steinbeck's *Tortilla Flat,* wanted to make a film from *The Red Pony* stories, presumably with Tracy in the most suitable role of Billy Buck. Steinbeck added that he would donate the rights to the stories and work on the script free if the others would also contribute their efforts so that all proceeds could be given to children in local hospitals. Fleming thought they might raise $2 million.

There is no evidence that Steinbeck did any work on a script at this time, and such wild-eyed philanthropy must have given fits to famed Metro-Goldwyn-Mayer studio boss Louis B. Mayer, to whom Fleming and Tracy were under contract, because the next year the studio would not even allow Tracy to read the over-voiced narration for *The Forgotten Village.* Steinbeck retaliated by threatening to take M-G-M to court if it used the name Jody in the film version of Marjorie Kinnan Rawlings's best-selling novel *The Yearling,* in which an unenthusiastic Tracy was scheduled to star. By the time *The Red Pony* was filmed, Steinbeck had changed his boy-hero's name to Tom. Joseph Millichap thinks that this change may have been made to avoid the name that had been used in *The Yearling,* but it seems more likely that by the time the film was made, Steinbeck wanted to use the name of his own first son Tom, born August 2, 1944

By April 1940 Steinbeck could advise Elizabeth Otis that arrangements were being made with Lewis Milestone (director of *Of Mice and Men,* one of the most impressive film versions of a Steinbeck novel) to film the story cycle, but financial problems had caused delays. By April 1940 they did have a contract with RKO (at the height of its prestige for Orson Welles's *Citizen Kane*) to make the film, and Steinbeck was preparing to write a synopsis, but production was delayed again, and the film did not materialize until after World War II when Milestone directed it at Republic Studios. Steinbeck did mention in 1941 that he was working with only three of the stories, and his concept of the story line may have been approaching its final form.

Since the film was not actually produced until 1949, there is another consideration in evaluating the final story line. During the long interval that the war delayed the project, Steinbeck had two sons of his own from his short-lived marriage to Gwyn Conger. Steinbeck made no secret when he was beginning work on what he considered his most ambitious novel, *East of Eden*, at about the same time *The Red Pony* was filmed, of his intention to dedicate the novel to providing some account of his own childhood background in the valleys and mountains around Salinas, California, for his sons when they were old enough to read and understand it. Certainly *The Red Pony* film could serve much the same purpose as an easier introductory work for the boys, so that the ultimate reason for his shaping the film script as he finally did could have been to provide a realistic but suitably entertaining and inspiring introduction to these childhood years for his own sons to enjoy when they were the age of the Tom in the film.

Steinbeck could exercise this kind of control over his project because by the time the film was shot on the Republic lot, the slowly dying company was serving principally as a distributor for independently produced films made by refugees from the old studio system who wanted to escape the domination of the exclusively profit-dominated New York bankers in order to produce what they considered works of artistic and humanistic value. . . .

Thus the backers of *The Red Pony* finally had a freedom in making the film that would have been impossible in the days when it was first conceived.

Unfortunately, Republic did not have very good distribution facilities, so that despite Steinbeck's reputation in 1949, the presence of such stars as Robert Mitchum and Myrna Loy in the cast, and the attraction of a soundtrack by the distinguished American composer Aaron Copeland, it was difficult to book first-run engagements in major cities. Reviewers were little help, for as Robert Morsberger observes, some of them found the modest, upbeat film "unexciting" at a time when the *film noirs*[3] that made stars like Robert Mitchum famous were all the rage. As a result, the film was not widely circulated, and for many years—after Republic Studios closed down—it was difficult to locate copies of it.

Perhaps videotape will now keep it permanently available as a minor but significant part of Steinbeck's work. It is one of those rare American films that proves it is possible to create well-crafted, dignified, emotionally moving films for preteenagers. Even if the film version does not do justice to the dramatic possibilities of the story cycle, the two offer an extraordinary opportunity to compare a major author's handling of the same basic story in two different media at two different points in his career.

3. dark films

CHRONOLOGY

1902

John Steinbeck born February 27

1903

Wright brothers make first manned airplane flight

1906

San Francisco earthquake and fire

1909

Steinbeck's sister Mary born; Model T Ford first mass-produced

1914

World War I begins in Europe; Panama Canal opens

1917

United States enters World War I

1919

Treaty of Versailles ending World War I; Steinbeck graduates from Salinas High School and enters Stanford University

1925

Steinbeck to New York, working as a laborer and as reporter for the *American* newspaper

1927

Charles Lindbergh's first solo transatlantic flight

1928

Talking pictures; first Mickey Mouse cartoon

1929

Stock market crash in America; Hoover becomes president; Steinbeck publishes *Cup of Gold*

1930

Steinbeck marries Carol Henning; meets Edward Ricketts in Pacific Grove

1932

Great Depression sweeps America; Charles Lindbergh Jr. kidnapped and murdered; Steinbeck publishes *Pastures of Heaven*

1933

Franklin D. Roosevelt becomes president; Steinbeck publishes *To a God Unknown*

1934

Steinbeck wins O. Henry Prize for "The Murder"; mother dies

1935

Works Progress Administration, work relief for unemployed; Steinbeck publishes *Tortilla Flat;* wins Commonwealth Club of California Gold Medal; Pascal Covici becomes Steinbeck's publisher

1936

Publishes *In Dubious Battle;* father dies; publishes articles on migrants in *San Francisco News*

1937

Publishes *Of Mice and Men;* wins Drama Critics' Circle Award; publishes *The Red Pony,* three parts

1938

Publishes *The Long Valley* and *Their Blood Is Strong,* a pamphlet based on news articles about migrants

1939

World War II begins in Europe; Steinbeck publishes *The Grapes of Wrath*

1940

Steinbeck and Ricketts's research trip to the Sea of Cortez; Steinbeck wins Pulitzer Prize for *The Grapes of Wrath;* films "The Forgotten Village" in Mexico; film versions of *The Grapes of Wrath* and *Of Mice and Men*

1941

Japanese bomb Pearl Harbor; America enters World War II; Steinbeck publishes *Sea of Cortez* with Ricketts

1942

Publishes *The Moon Is Down;* writes script for *Bombs Away;* Steinbeck and Carol Henning divorce; film version of *Tortilla Flat*

1943

Steinbeck marries Gwyndolen Conger; they move to New York; film version of *The Moon is Down;* to Europe as war correspondent for the New York *Herald-Tribune*

1944

D day invasion of Normandy; Steinbeck writes script for *Lifeboat* with Alfred Hitchcock; son Thomas born

1945

Franklin D. Roosevelt dies; Harry Truman becomes president; Americans drop first atomic bomb on Hiroshima; World War II ends; Steinbeck publishes *Cannery Row, The Red Pony,* in four parts, and "The Pearl of the World" in *Woman's Home Companion*

1946

First meeting of the United Nations; son John born

1947

Publishes *The Wayward Bus* and *The Pearl;* goes to Russia with photographer Robert Capa

1948

Berlin blockage and airlift; Steinbeck publishes *A Russian Journal;* elected to American Academy of Letters; film version of *The Pearl;* Edward Ricketts dies; Steinbeck and Gwyndolen Conger divorce

1949

Film version of *The Red Pony*

1950

America involved in Korean War; Steinbeck publishes *Burning Bright,* novel and play; writes script for *Viva Zapata!;* marries Elaine Scott

1951

Publishes *Log from the Sea of Cortez*

1952

Publishes *East of Eden*

1953

Dwight D. Eisenhower becomes president

1954

Publishes *Sweet Thursday*

1957

Publishes *The Short Reign of Pippin IV;* film version of *The Wayward Bus*

1958

Publishes *Once There Was a War*

1959

Alaska admitted as the forty-ninth state; Hawaii admitted as fiftieth

1960

Steinbeck tours America with dog Charley

1961

John F. Kennedy becomes president; Soviets build Berlin Wall; first U.S. manned suborbital flight; Steinbeck publishes *The Winter of Our Discontent*

1962

Cuban missile crisis; Steinbeck publishes *Travels with Charley in Search of America*; awarded Nobel Prize in literature

1963

John F. Kennedy assassinated; Lyndon Johnson becomes president

1964–1975

America involved in Vietnam War

1965

Reports from Vietnam for *Newsday*

1966

Publishes *America for Americans*

1968

Martin Luther King assassinated; televised versions of *Travels with Charley, Of Mice and Men,* and *The Grapes of Wrath;* Steinbeck dies on December 20; buried in Salinas

1969

Richard M. Nixon becomes president; publication of *Journal of a Novel: The* East of Eden *Letters*

1970

Opera version of *Of Mice and Men*

1975

Steinbeck: A Life in Letters, edited by Elaine Steinbeck and Robert Wallstein

FOR FURTHER RESEARCH

ABOUT JOHN STEINBECK AND *THE RED PONY*

Richard Astro and Tetsumaro Hayashi, eds., *Steinbeck: The Man and His Work*. Proceedings of the 1970 Steinbeck Conference, sponsored by Oregon State and Ball State Universities. Corvallis: Oregon State University Press, 1971.

Jackson J. Benson, *The True Adventures of John Steinbeck, Writer*. New York: Viking, 1984.

Warren French, *John Steinbeck*. New York: Twayne, 1961.

Maxwell Geismar, *Writers in Crisis: The American Novel, 1925–1945*. Boston: Houghton Mifflin, 1942.

James Gray, *John Steinbeck*. Pamphlets on American Writers, no. 94. Minneapolis: University of Minnesota Press, 1971.

Tetsumaro Hayashi, ed., *A Study Guide to John Steinbeck: A Handbook to His Major Works*. Metuchen, NJ: Scarecrow Press, 1974.

Frederick J. Hoffman, *The Modern Novel in America*. Chicago: Henry Regnery, 1951.

Alfred Kazin, *On Native Grounds: An Interpretation of Modern American Prose Literature*. New York: Harcourt, Brace & World, 1942.

Thomas Kiernan, *The Intricate Music: A Biography of John Steinbeck*. Boston: Little, Brown, 1979.

Peter Lisca, *The Wide World of John Steinbeck*. New Brunswick, NJ: Rutgers University Press, 1958.

Jay Parini, *John Steinbeck: A Biography*. New York: Henry Holt, 1995.

John Steinbeck, *The Short Novels of John Steinbeck: Tortilla Flat, The Red Pony, Of Mice and Men, The Moon Is Down, Cannery Row, The Pearl*. Edited and with Introduction by Joseph Henry Jackson. New York: Viking, 1953.

E.W. Tedlock Jr. and C.V. Wicker, eds., *Steinbeck and His Critics: A Record of Twenty-Five Years*. Albuquerque: University of New Mexico Press, 1957.

Arthur Voss, *The American Short Story: A Critical Survey.* Norman: University of Oklahoma Press, 1973.

ABOUT STEINBECK'S TIMES

Frederick Lewis Allen, *Since Yesterday: The Nineteen-Thirties in America, September 3, 1929–September 3, 1939.* New York: Harper & Brothers, 1940.

Jules Archer, *The Incredible Sixties: The Stormy Years that Changed America.* San Diego: Harcourt Brace Jovanovich, 1986.

Robert C. Cotner, John S. Ezell, and Gilbert C. Fete, *Readings in American History.* Vol. 2, *1865–Present.* Boston: Houghton Mifflin, 1952.

Matthew T. Downey et al., eds., *The Great Depression and World War II (1930–1945).* Vol. 3 of *The Twentieth Century.* New York: Macmillan, 1992.

John Kenneth Galbraith, *The Great Crash: 1929.* Boston: Houghton Mifflin, 1961.

Milton Meltzer, *Brother, Can You Spare a Dime: The Great Depression: 1929–1933.* New York: Knopf, 1969.

Douglas T. Miller and Marion Nowak, *The Fifties: The Way We Really Were.* Garden City, NY: Doubleday, 1977.

Allan Nevins and Henry Steele Commager with Jeffrey Morris, *A Pocket History of the United States.* 9th rev. ed. New York: Pocket Books, 1986.

Teresa O'Neill, ed., *The Great Depression: Opposing Viewpoints.* American History Series. San Diego: Greenhaven, 1994.

Martin Ridge and Ray Allen Billington, eds., *America's Frontier Story.* New York: Holt, Rinehart and Winston, 1969.

Jerry Stanley, *Children of the Dust Bowl: The True Story of the School at Weedpatch Camp.* New York: Crown, 1992.

Ted Tuleja, *American History in 100 Nutshells.* New York: Faucett Columbine, 1992.

Howard Zinn, *A People's History of the United States.* New York: Harper Perennial, Division of Harper Collins, 1980.

INDEX

Abramson, Ben, 19
Albee, Richard, 48
Allee, W.C., 48
archetypes, 130–31
"Argument of Phalanx,"
 48–49
Astro, Richard, 46
Athens and Jerusalem
 (Shestov), 102
*Autobiography, The Descent
 of Man* (Darwin), 40
awards
 New York Drama Critics'
  Circle Award, 20
 Nobel Prize, 27, 41, 77
 O. Henry Award, 19
 Pulitzer Prize, 24

Bartlett, Randolph, 108
Benson, Jackson J., 12, 21,
 26, 41
Benton, Robert M., 73
*Bombs Away: The Story of a
 Bomber*, 25
Buck, Billy, 70
 on American pioneer past,
  67
 approaches ideal hero,
  43–45
 cares for sick pony, 29
 contrasted with Carl Tiflin,
  70, 74

on dead buzzard, 82–83
on death of mice, 68
delivers colt, 32, 71–72, 76,
 88–89
educates Jody, 81
in film version, 117, 119,
 123, 132–33
helps Jody train, 28
imperfection in, 82
Jody fashions himself
 after, 64
Jody's trust in, 111
as man of skill, 66
as substitute father, 87, 93
tension through, 100
Burning Bright, 25, 137

Cady, Edwin H., 59
Calhern, Louis, 117
Cannery Row, 24
 ending of, 137
 man of skill in, 66
 revised, 26
Capa, Robert, 24
Champney, Freeman, 35
characters, 28
 in film version, 117
 see also specific characters
"Chrysanthemums, The,"
 66–67
Conger, Gwendolyn (wife),
 22, 24, 25

Copeland, Aaron, 118
Covici, Pascal, 19–20
Cup of Gold, A, 16, 17, 137–38

Darwin, Charles
  on animals vs. humans, 39
  on humility, 40–41
  presents the truth, 42–43
  on sympathy, 41–42
death
  buzzards symbolize, 83–84
  cypress tree symbolizes,
    54, 70, 100–101
  of Gitano, 64–65, 74–75
  imperfection and, 80, 82, 86
  Jody's fascination with, 84
  Jody's initiation into
    adulthood through, 70
  as a natural process, 65
  as part of rhythmic cycle,
    53–54, 91
  as search for origins, 85
"Death of the Hired Man,
  The" (Frost), 116
Dennis, Wesley, 118
Descent of Man, The
  (Darwin), 42
Duvivier, Julien, 129

East of Eden, 26, 137, 139

Fadiman, Clifton, 110
Farewell to Arms , A
  (Hemingway), 52–53
Fleming, Victor, 138
Flesh and Fantasy (film), 129
Fonda, Henry, 22
Forgotten Village, The
  (film), 25, 138
  contrasted with *The Red
    Pony* film, 136–37
  group behavior in, 47
French, Warren, 59, 126
Frost, Robert, 116

Frye, Northrop, 130–31

Gaither, Gloria, 57
Gaudio, Tony, 118
Gide, André, 112
"Gifts of Ivan, The," 17
Gitano
  Carl's cruelty toward, 30,
    64, 75, 92
  death of, as calm and
    peaceful, 64
  as extension of mountains,
    55–56
  father of, compared with
    Jody's father, 86
  influence of, on Jody,
    30–31, 64–65, 71, 75, 111,
    116
  searches for origins, 84–85
Goldsmith, Arnold L., 51
grandfather
  Carl's cruelty toward, 32,
    33, 76, 92–93, 116
  in film version, 120–22,
    133
  Jody's education through,
    63, 66–68, 76–77
  Jody's maturation through,
    98–100
  see also westering
Grapes of Wrath, The, 22
  communion with nature in,
    55
  film version of, 135
  individual and group
    relationships in, 50
  Pulitzer Prize for, 24
Graves, Glenn, 14
Gregory, Susan, 19

Hamilton, Margaret, 122
Harper's, 126
Hart, Richard E., 57
Hemingway, Ernest, 51–52,

52–53
Henning, Carol, 17
Herald-Tribune (New York), 24
Hitchcock, Alfred, 25
Hooker, J.D., 42
Hyman, Stanley Edgar, 57

imagery
  buzzards, 82
  stallion, 87–88
"Indian Camp" (Hemingway), 53
In Dubious Battle, 19, 137–38
Ingram, Forrest L., 127

Johnson, Lyndon, 27

Kaufman, George S., 20
Kazan, Elia, 137
Kennedy, John F., 27
Kennedy, John S., 48
Kline, Herbert, 136

"Lady in Infra-Red, A," 16
Levant, Howard, 79
Lifeboat (film), 25
Lisca, Peter, 63
Log from the Sea of Cortez, 58–59
Long Valley, The, 50, 77, 110
Lorentz, Pare, 136
Loy, Myrna, 117, 139
Lyell, Sir Charles, 42

McIntosh, Mavis, 19
McWilliams, Carey, 36, 38
Miles, Peter, 117
Milestone, Lewis, 114, 138
Miller, Ted, 16
Millichap, Joseph R., 114, 134, 138
Mirrielees, Edith, 16, 17
Mitchum, Robert, 117, 139

Moon Is Down, The, 24, 137
Moore, Harry Thornton, 104, 106
Mors, George, 15
Morsberger, Robert, 139–40
"Murder, The," 19, 66–67

narrative
  descriptive detail in, 74, 95–96
  in film version, 118
  intimate knowledge through, 109
  and Jody's point of view, 79–80, 88–89
  suggests imperfection, 81
  see also style
Nation, 21
nature
  Buck's lessons on, 43–45
  in film version, 118, 122
  free will and, 59–61
  as impersonal, 82, 83
  Jody learns from, 63, 74
  man as part of, 58–59
  mystical connections with, 55–56
  as neutral, 80
  Steinbeck's connection with, 12
  Steinbeck's treatment of, 57–58
Newsday, 27
New York Drama Critics' Circle Award, 20
New Yorker, 110
New York Times Book Review, 110
Nobel Prize in literature, 27, 41, 77
North American Review, 19, 20, 126

Of Mice and Men, 20

ending of, 137–38
film version of, 22, 114
naturalism in, 59
stage version of, 20
O. Henry Award, 19
Osterling, Anders, 57
Otis, Elizabeth, 19, 27, 138

Parini, Jay, 12–13, 15, 110
  on Steinbeck at Lake
    Tahoe, 16–17
  on Steinbeck's fame, 20
  on Steinbeck's Nobel Prize
    speech, 27
Pastures of Heaven, 18, 19,
  103, 137–38
Pearl, The, 24–25, 137
plot, 28–33, 73–74, 108–109,
  115–16, 127–29
Pulitzer Prize, 24

"Raid, The," 19
Railsback, Brian E., 39
Red Pony, The (film version),
  114–15
  alterations from book in,
    124–25, 129–30, 132–33
  birth of colt in, 124
  characters in, 117
  contrasted with "The
    Forgotten Village," 136–37
  difficulties in adaptation of,
    117
  distribution of, 139–40
  ending of, 137–38
  evaluation of, 134–35
  Hollywood formula in,
    133–34
  from idea to filming,
    138–39
  music in, 118
  opening for, 118–19
  pony's illness and death in,
    122–24

red pony and grandfather
  story combined in, 120–22
setting in, 118
story cycle in, 131–32
Ricketts, Edward
  death of, 25
  on individual and group
    relationships, 46–47, 49
  influence of, on Steinbeck's
    writing, 19
  Steinbeck's friendship with,
    15, 18
  travels with Steinbeck,
    25–26
Rohrenberg, Mary, 112
Russian Journal, The, 24, 25

Salinas Valley, 106
  extremes of wealth and
    poverty in, 38
  major occupations , 36
  physical description of, 35
  Steinbeck on, 12
  Steinbeck's intimate
    knowledge with, 52
  see also setting
Scott, Elaine (wife), 25–26
Scott, Waverly, 25
Sea of Cortez, 55, 57, 65–66
setting
  descriptive detail of, 95
  in film version, 118, 124–25
  symbolism in, 116
  see also Salinas Valley
Sheffield, Duke, 16
Shestov, Lev, 102
*Short Reign of Pippin IV, a
  Fabrication, The*, 26
Smith, Elizabeth, 16, 17
Smoker's Companion, 17
Spectator, 16
"Spring and Fall: To a Young
  Child" (Hopkins), 65
Stanford University, 15–16

Steinbeck, Carol (wife),
    21–22, 24
Steinbeck, Elizabeth (sister),
    12, 16
Steinbeck, Esther (sister), 12
Steinbeck, John (son), 24
Steinbeck, John Ernst, Jr.
    agrees with Darwin, 39
    childhood of, 12–13, 14–15
    death of, 27
    on Gabilan Mountains, 98
    humility of, 41
    marriages of, 17–18, 24,
        25–26
    on migrant workers, 21–22
    Nobel Prize speech by, 27
    on *The Red Pony* film
        version, 135
    shyness of, 13–14
    Stanford years of, 15–16
    on sympathy, 42
    travels of, 25, 26–27
    writing by
        critical reviews of, 26, 57
        depicting highest human
            in, 39–40, 42–43
        early success of, 19–20
        for films, 25, 114–15,
            135–37
        first failures of, 18–19
        free will and nature in,
            59–61
        individual and group
            relationships in, 46,
            47–48
        on migrant workers, 22
        mystical connections with
            nature in, 55
        naturalism in, 57–60
        and paper on group
            behavior, 48–49
        and *The Red Pony* film
            version, 138–39
        and short stories vs. long

        fiction, 112
        at Stanford, 16–17
        on war, 24
        on writing *The Red Pony*,
            73, 91
Steinbeck, John Ernest, Sr.
    (father), 12, 14
Steinbeck, Mary (sister), 14
Steinbeck, Olivia Hamilton
    (mother), 12, 14, 19
Steinbeck, Thom (son), 24
Steinbeck Review, 57
structure
    archetypal pattern in,
        130–31
    in film version, 129–30,
        131–33
    and interrelationship of
        stories, 128–29
    life-death cycle in, 53–54,
        91
    and self-contained
        novelettes, 108–109
    and tension, 100–102
    through seasons and times
        of day, 90–91
    and time sequence, 52–53,
        90
    and unity of episodes, 79–80
    see also style
Strudwick, Shepperd, 117
style
    and distance of characters,
        63–64
    and new prose, 105, 107
Sweet Thursday, 26
symbolism
    of buzzards, 80, 83–84
    of cypress tree, 54, 70,
        100–101
    of death of westering, 68
    of life and death rhythms,
        53–54
    of mountains/Gitano,

55–56, 70–71
phallic, 85
of rain, 52–53
of red pony, 115
in setting, 116
of Tiflin ranch, 64
of water tub, 54, 56, 70,
  101–102

Tahoe, Lake, 16–17
Tales of Manhattan, 129
Taylor, Jess, 28, 30
  reader's distance from,
    63–64
themes
  death and fatherhood,
    84–85
  education of Jody, 63–68
  illness and death, 82
  imperfection and death,
    82–84, 86
  imperfection combined
    with happiness, 80–82
  individual and group
    relationships, 50
  Jody's maturation, 79,
    102–103
  life-death cycle, 53–54
  loss, acceptance, and
    growth, 69, 70, 91
  man and nature
    relationship, 59
  trust, 111
Tiflin, Carl, 69–70
  on American pioneer past,
    67
  Billy Buck substitutes, 87
  contrasted with Billy Buck,
    70, 74
  on dead buzzard, 29,
    82–83
  as father, compared with
    Gitano's father, 85–86
  in film version, 117, 120,

121–22
  gift of colt by, 31, 96
  gift of red pony by, 28
  on Gitano, 30, 64, 71, 75,
    85–86
  on grandfather, 32, 33, 76,
    92–93, 116
  imperfections of, 80–81
  lack of visionary dreaming
    by, 96–97, 98
  pragmatism in, 93–94
  as stern and unbending,
    92, 94
  wisdom of, 43
Tiflin, Jody
  as autobiographical
    character, 105
  awareness of imperfection
    in, 82–83, 86, 88–89
  on birth of colt, 31–32, 111
    and education, 65, 75–76
    in film version, 124
    and initiation into
      adulthood, 71–72
  communion with nature
    by, 55
  at cypres tree, 100–102
  descriptive details about,
    95–96
  and fantasy games, 86–87
  in film version (as Tom),
    117, 119–20, 133–34, 138
  on grandfather/westering,
    32–33
    and education, 66–68,
      76–77
    in film version, 119–20,
      122
    and initiation into
      adulthood, 72
    and maturation, 98–100,
      112, 116
    and visionary dreaming,
      98–99

on great mountains/Gitano, 29–31, 55–56, 115–16
and education, 64–65, 74–75
and fatherhood, 84–85
and initiation into adulthood, 70–71
and maturation, 111, 115–16
and visionary dreaming, 97–98
and happiness over red pony, 81
learns ranch life, 66
maturation of, 91, 102
rebels against father, 91–95
on red pony's death, 29
and education, 64, 74
in film version, 122–24
and initiation into adulthood, 70
and maturation, 83–84, 110–11, 115
similarities in, and Hemingway character, 51–52
trains red pony, 28–29, 121
as wise vs. gay, 106
Tiflin, Ruth, 31, 70, 81
in film version, 117, 120
on grandfather's stories, 67, 112
Timmerman, John H., 90
To a God Unknown, 18, 19, 103
Tortilla Flat
ending of, 137–38

film version of, 20, 135
publication of, 19–20
Tracy, Spencer, 22, 138
Travels with Charley in Search of America, 27
True Adventures of John Steinbeck, Writer, The (Benson), 12, 41
Turner, Frederick Jackson, 116

Vietnam War, 27
Viva Zapata! (film), 25, 137

Wagner, Max, 14
Watt, F.W., 69
Wayward Bus, The, 25, 137
westering, 32–33
death of, 68, 116
individual and group relationships in, 50
Jody's maturation through, 72, 98–100
nature and free will in, 61
see also grandfather
Whipple, T.K., 63
"White Quail, The," 20
Wilhelmson, Carl, 17, 18–19
Williams, Annie Laurie, 110
Winter of Our Discontent, The, 26
Woodward, Robert H., 44

Young, Stanley, 110

Zapata, Emiliano, 137